THE ABSURDITY OF DOING YOU

Rebel
Elegance
for the
Evolving
Soul

THE ABSURDITY OF DOING YOU

JANINE NICOLE DENNIS

atmosphere press

Published by Atmosphere Press

Cover design by Matthew Fielder

atmospherepress.com

TABLE of CONTENTS

LET'S SET AN INTENTION

This book is incredibly special to me. It is the first time in my life that I have felt comfortable sharing this much of myself and my life with the world. I have learned many lessons throughout my thirty-nine years on this planet and I want it to stand for something. It is my hope that this book defies every single law in the universe while simultaneously grounding you, the reader, in the order of our existence. This book personifies a paradoxical and perhaps absurd way of thinking, but then we must remember the title of the book.

As you read the book, my intention and wish for you is that you see the collective story, every individual anecdote, and stream of consciousness in this book as a call to action to not only consume what is written but actively engage with it and apply it to your life. You will find prompts that are delivered as summaries of what you read. Equally, you will encounter questions to make you think about your own life and your unique expression of it. I encourage you to be an active reader and courageous in making this book your own. Regard me as a trusted guide while you navigate the variety of topics I cover here. My goal with this book was to tell my story, my way, but more importantly to be of help.

I am granting you a golden key of sorts to unlocking

hidden truths of life within my story. Now that you are going to be privy to all of my business, we're friends. Whether you read this from end to end, skim it for the juicy chapters, or keep it as a piece of artistry in your favorite space being called to read when your spirit is moved to do so, I love you for taking this journey with me. I am with you with every page turn and every prompt cheering you on to be rebellious, absurd, and brutally honest about what makes you who you are.

Let's begin!

Much love,
Janine

WELCOME TO MY EXOPLANET

Everything in life and society coaxes us to be anything but ourselves. I know this because I am one of the few that has chosen to defy convention rather than become it. Of course, I started out like so many others, steeped in all the rules, niceties, and generational and societal ways of being until I awakened to an echo-chamber world where likeness and dare I say "whiteness" was the norm and oddities were anomalies of the human condition. After 38 years of human experience, I've concluded that the sooner we detox ourselves from the conditioning, expectations, and false narratives, the sooner we can get on with living our most absurd, audacious, and beautiful life. It is fair to acknowledge that this path is a divine offering to every human regardless of race, creed, religion, sexuality, insert your aesthetic of choice, but only a select group of souls grab at the opportunity. It is my belief that this life is nothing more than a quantum moment of absurdity, lessons, and evolution. Should you choose to buy into my beliefs, you ought to consider this as well; Life is a series of blessings within the blessing. It is my job throughout the course of this book to illustrate how I have come to this conclusion about life and why you should live out yours in the most absurd, rebellious, and meaningful manner for you. Life isn't so much about achieving something as it is about the learning, unlearning, discovering of your "all-spark," and evolution of the soul. In a nutshell, life is a progression towards leaving a unique mark on humanity.

This is my story and my perspective.

TOUGH LOVE

Are you not concerned that perhaps none of what you have become, nor anything you currently do is authentically you? The story you're about to read is wholly mine, but what about you?

How long will you choose to be deluded by societal frameworks, familial conditioning, fears projected upon you, and decision-making that on the surface looks like it is working for you, but at the core of your being you know is sending you billions of lightyears away from your true essence?

We are living during one of the biggest social experiments known to man. In a mere two years, "the powers that be" have managed to inject us global citizens with an extremely precise dosage of censorship, sickness, fear, and conditioning. When we look back on the top of the '20s, it will be crystal clear that your sovereignty was squandered for control and in some cases your luxuries depending on the decisions you made. You will find that your decisions weren't necessarily made with the greater good in mind at all, but rather with your greatest fear, the fear of being no more. Death is a readily available foe, very much misunderstood and explored reluctantly. Yet, our governments and media outlets have had it on full display and blaring into your homes daily for the better half of two years.

In a culture that prides itself on being progressively more and more conscious of every citizen's needs and increasingly more sensitive to everyone's humanity, you have to ask yourself where humanity was in traumatizing citizens around the clock with your greatest fear. You will have to admit that perhaps you trusted rank and file more than you trusted yourself and quite frankly your fellow human. What may have waxed poetic and even intelligent while you were in the quagmire dis-ease in the wake of this great reset, will dial up questions about your mental health and how you strayed so far from your normative existence that you decided you thought you knew what was best for others too.

What a mind-fuck this will all be for us all when you realize a million different things were true and false all at once, but you allowed your ego to get the best of you. There it is, memorialized both in real life and digitally, a human in ruin, unaware of the ways you were being manipulated and woefully unaware of your higher calling. The truth is both inconvenient and uncomfortable when you have been trained your entire life to sift and compartmentalize information in self-serving ways, perpetuating your dogma and narratives, and ultimately feeding your biases.

I urge you all to assume you don't know much. Consider that all your formal education and life experience has maybe scratched the surface of what there is to know in this life. Your ability to think clearly and prismatically is as necessary as the air you breathe. In my humble opinion, anyone who would give their freedom away wantonly and spread information hastily in the absence of a higher, measured, yet broader perspective is a dangerous person and certainly no one I can have in close proximity to me or my family. Unbeknownst to the individual, a person like this is chaotic and not making full use of the hardware humans come aptly equipped with. Plainly, you are dangerous because you've not mastered your mind or spirit. You are easily swayed by what the populace offers in mindset and behavior, but leery of your own heart, intellect, and intuition. Who can you be of assistance to in this state? The answer is no one. Your operating system has many corrupted files that have the look and appearance of normal algorithms, but that is an illusion.

To know me is to know that I see things for exactly what they are and the multitude of things they could be. I see all possibilities and all deficits which allow me to give every human and every circumstance the grace of being exactly as it is, standing naked in all its unwavering existence and true essence. I'm inviting you all back to the truth, for it never cheats us. Allow what I share in this book to wash over you, let it make love to your neurons and synapses. Then, go be in nature, get still. Start to synthesize what comes up for you and decide what needs to shift within you.

If this was triggering to read, I'm glad. It means I am doing what I was designed to do, however absurd. It's all love, but I wouldn't be doing my job with this book if I didn't highlight the war at play. It isn't the war that first crossed your mind, but rather something more personal. We are at war with ourselves. One of the more poignant references of the "war" I am speaking of is illustrated in Bob Marley's song "War." Essentially, he says throughout the song that everywhere we look there is war. He doubles down in an almost weary, but passionate way to say that the consistent war within humanity will never be over until our philosophies of needing one human to be inferior to another and our illusions of superiority are "discredited and abandoned" completely and basic human rights are afforded to everyone. Baba Marley is not just referring to "everyone" from an "All Lives Matter" standpoint but does the song justice by highlighting that most of our collective debt is due to people of the African diaspora who have been the recipients of evil acts and immoral systems and structures. For those who know more about Bob Marley and are having a philosophical issue with his lyrics and how he lived his life, know that I, too, am aware of his imperfections and inconsistencies. Nonetheless, it doesn't detract from the valiant way he spoke or illustrated the atrocities of our time through music. It's about the message more than the messenger for me. I hope by the end of this book you become more expansive about how you not only see yourself, but other imperfect messengers.

This is only the beginning. I look forward to being a trusty companion throughout this book, lovingly yet sternly guiding you to manage that which is in your sphere of influence.

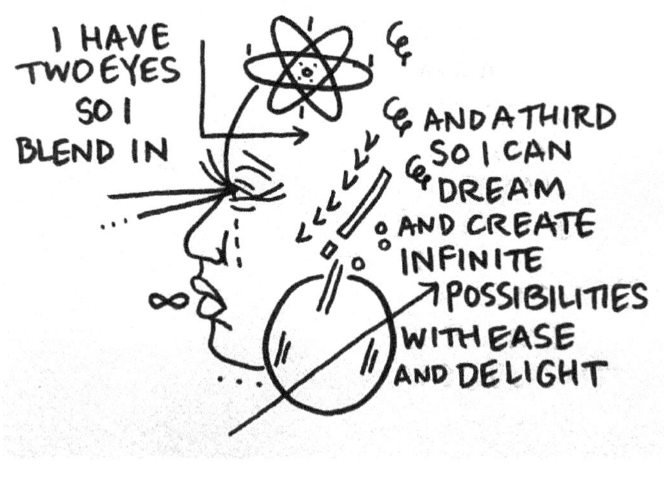

THE POWER OF MANIFESTATION

How do you change your reality? You become contemplative and remember your power.

The tragedy of humanity is we don't use nearly half of the star power within us. One of the gifts I have been most grateful for has been my ability to manifest the reality I want. Some call it prayers and yet others call it manifestations. It is this act of intentionally thinking about the things you desire and the experiences you want to have by pairing them with the way you want to feel upon receipt of the blessing. The key is these manifestations must come from a heart of gratitude, even if all you can muster is a mustard seed of it. They must be genuinely dressed with a positive outlook on your life, with an excitement for what is possible, and a reverence for what is currently present for you.

This book is one of my wildest dreams...manifestations, prayers. It started with people asking me when I would write a book. Most who asked posed the question as if the natural course of my career and life dictated that a book must happen. In most industries, a book is a powerful signal that you have somehow made it and are worthy of the public domain's attention. It must be said that often the rush to drop a book garners our attention even when what is being said is far from compelling, evolutionary, or revolutionary.

To that end, I was never in a rush to put a book out to satisfy the palates of colleagues or to even keep up with them. From this notion alone, you can start to see why the book is titled as it is. I don't have a care in the world to move to the beat and cadence of anyone else's drum. I wrote this book on planes, in airport terminals while waiting for flights, in hotel rooms in a variety of cities, on a laptop, on my phone, in multiple journals, and in living the unfolding, unraveling, and becoming of an unconventional, uncomfortable, otherworldly, extraordinary life to date.

I wrote this book because it was already written in the stars for me to do so. The flesh is weak, but my intuition, divine guidance, and timing is all. I am moved by my spirit more than the words and urging of man. When the visibility and opportunity to write this book came during one of the most chaotic years and amidst so much change and transition in my life, I knew I would be challenged, uncomfortable, and stretched in ways I couldn't even imagine. I was cracked wide open writing this book and dreaming this dream. This is freedom and this is my truth. I've had to care enough to say things in such a way that I didn't harm anybody, but also not care enough to say what is true so I could free myself. I accepted that challenge all the same.

Here's a short story about how we arrived here with this title and book for you to stimulate your neurons and synapses with.

May 22nd, 2015 was the day the title of my book came to me. Specifically, it was during one of my late-night breast-feeding sessions that year that my then best friend Melissa said, "Ni-ni, you need to write a book." At that time, we used to keep each other company, talking about the mundane to the scholarly aspects of life while breastfeeding our boys until the wee hours of the morning. We discussed at least three to four companies we could build together during those sessions as well, but this book was one that stuck. That day, I put a note in my Evernote titled "Book title ideas."

Later that day, I meditated on the idea of me writing a book. This was courageous seeing as though 2015 was one of the hardest years of my life. I call it my "year of tears." After that meditation, the title of the book came to me: "The Absurdity of Doing You." I rushed to find my phone to add it to my Evernote as I had goosebumps and chills thinking about the promise of this title.

I said to myself, in a few years you will write a book detailing everything you are experiencing now, so it is the right time to chronicle a list of titles. Fast forward over five years and "The Absurdity of Doing You: Rebel Elegance for the Evolving Soul" is here.

I wrote this down. I followed my intuition and I let it go. Here's a tip. The most powerful prayers and manifestations come true when we refine our intentions, wants, and needs and we have an unwavering belief in the universe (insert your all-knowing power of choice) to bring about our heart's desire. We don't keep praying because that is based in fear and lack of trust. We pray and let it go. We let go with the same unwavering beliefs we had when making a wish and blowing on a dandelion as a child or throwing a penny in the wishing well. The joy is in the surprise and serendipity of your prayer's unique timing. Just when you least expect it, a blessing is born, and that manifestation is no longer an undying yearning but your reality. Pretty cool.

> ***Evolving Soul Reflection:*** *Don't dismiss the urgings of your heart, messages, premonitions, or ideas that come to you intuitively. They are seeds yet to germinate. You will hear me say this in different ways throughout this book. Everything happens for your*

good in divine time. Your job is to hold true to your vision, remain faithful, and stay the course, all while spinning and rotating on the axis of your very own exoplanet.

"REDEFINING HUMAN-BEING"

March 18th, 2020

I must admit that I understand the hysteria surrounding this virus, but I don't resonate with it. People are looking for more snippets and soundbites that will make them feel better about an occurrence that is about to reset our lives as we know it. It is okay to feel sad, scared, anxious, and uneasy, and yet all those emotions have always called us to acknowledge them and then heal. We were never in control of our livelihoods, the way the economy may unfold, or an infectious disease. Nonetheless, the evidence of everything that was crumbling slowly but surely was right under our noses. We didn't care about any of it, because we were too busy securing bags, traveling, being unkind to ourselves and others, destroying the environment, expecting to have groceries 24/7/365, because clearly the Earth is never tired of supplying our inordinate number of wants. This generation of sentient beings has never had a healthy relationship with want vs. need. We have to admit that we have an even unhealthier relationship with the finite nature of our lives and stillness. We will survive this, as others have faced similar catastrophes in the past. Get real about what is happening and why you feel foreign in your own body while we try to tame this beast.

A tough love word for you all...

We all have emotions, feelings, and thoughts. We are hard wired to have a myriad of all of them in response to things we perceive as "bad." During this time of stillness and hopefully, mindfulness, you will consider the following:

1. We are all here on a finite journey. There was a beginning and so an end shall follow. The day or hour when our particular instance is over is above our pay grade. Let us make the most of our moments no matter how short they may seem.

2. We have experiences. They are neither intended to be good or bad. They are merely instances to advance your soul's knowing and understanding of what it is to be human. These are lessons, if you will. If you look back on all of your life lessons to date, you will admit that they all weren't especially pleasant, but they were useful.

3. Use this time of transition to retreat and get educated about the true nature of the world we have all been paying into with our money, talents, and psyches. The goal post signs of our irresponsible impact on one another and the Earth have been front and center for a long time now. Being angry with those who awakened beyond the many illusions you are tethered to is fruitless. Take this as an opportunity to learn and evaluate why the truth is so foreign to you.

It's time to take responsibility for your life, own your decisions, and realize that our first priorities are to be well, mind, body, and spirit, and then see that our fellow human brethren do the same.

Welcome to being human.

We missed you.

I wrote this when we were a mere few days into shelter-in-place here in New York in 2020. I knew 2020 would be a defining moment in 2019. For the better part of the 2010s, I would tell my mom that the pace we were all traveling in life and at work was unsustainable. The "normal" everyone is so eager to return to was far from normal; in fact, it was a little slice of hell if you believe in that sort of thing. Children weren't skipping off to school with glee. The U.S. education system needs to crumble so it can be a source of inspiration for our youth rather than a source of degradation. Adults were overworked and unhappy in their work environments for the most part. How does that living make for a good life? Instead of redesigning work to fit the circumstances we were all faced with, most employers found new ways to destroy their employees; only this time, it was in the one place where you should be safe...your home. We will be wondering in the years and decades to come how we got bamboozled into working and operating as if normal during mass hysteria, due to a virus whose spread continues to evade both the intellect and grasp of our elected officials, has sustained death tolls globally, incited civil unrest, and peppered us with political upheaval. We were woefully blind to the atrocities that lay in plain sight for decades. I'd like to think we are far more aware of the injustices and insanity that we have been consciously and unconsciously been funding with our capital and with our apathy for the oppressed.

We are not very good human beings. We are masterful human-doings preoccupied with greed, illusions, power, and prestige. We're an unhealthy society with parasitic minds and compromised spirits. Don't look for data in this book to back my bold assertions; the proof is inherent in the statement and illustrated quite vividly all around you should you want to acknowledge it.

I've taken the time to get to know myself, so I may understand my place in this world better. In doing so, I hope it encourages you to do the same. If we all take the time to be students of our own lives, we will find that the answers of our respective and collective purpose become clearer and our call to action louder. Sure, "The Absurdity of Doing You" chronicles my life story so far, with the hope of getting you to see your own differently and hopefully with greater reverence.

More importantly, it is a book designed to illuminate the many prongs of modern life that need our awareness and our hearts committed to creating a better human blueprint for future generations to aspire to.

> ***Evolving Soul Reflection:*** *One thing to know about me, I am plenty brainy. I think about things, and I try to dissect them often. One of my pet peeves is the lack of critical and free thinking in our current society. We must believe that even with all of our complex functionality, big brains, and consciousness, we haven't exactly been the best species. We have gotten so bad, in fact, that the only way we seem to accept change is via suffering and trauma. 2020 was a huge reset for the human race. We are the magicians on this rotating rock. We can either envision and build something way better than "normal," or we can stay tethered to a past that is never returning in our lifetime and seems comfortable to romanticize because we are too cowardly to traverse a wild card present and future.*
>
> *Your alignment with your own evolution and purpose starts here. In this book, you will find a variety of stories and reflections shared with the intention of making you reflect on how you are showing up in your own life. Take some time to reflect on how you are feeling in your human body today. What comes up for you? How has your overall outlook on life changed since 2020?*

Use the space below to document your evolving soul reflections.

THE BLUEPRINT

My blueprint is colorful and complex. I am woven from a unique fabric that I am certain they don't make any more. From the beginning of my existence, you couldn't tell me I wasn't a fully grown person. In hindsight, I can totally see and acknowledge that I was once a little person, but I never felt that way inside, and no one ever treated me as such until it suited them. In fact, there hasn't been a day I can remember where I didn't feel like an adult holding the weight of the universe on my back. We all come into the world with a placenta attached. I am convinced I came in with the placenta fully equipped with a stealthy ball and chain. The point is: From an early age, I felt extremely responsible for the well-being of others. This is also an effect of being too smart for your own good. I excelled in school, sure, but the "smarts" I am referring to extended to my very keen understanding of the world and the humans in it. Sometimes, I think I might have been better off playing ignorant, but alas I could not help myself. As a result, my unique lens and awareness of the world reared its head early and astutely. From that point on, people have relied upon my advanced understanding of people, circumstances, and life.

This sense and presence carried into my pre-teen years

and adolescence as I became more and more of an enigma for my peers, a challenge for my parents, and euphoric confusion in my own head as I had already decided who and what I was going to be in this world.

It hasn't always been fun and jokes in my head to run mental laps around adults twice my age. By the time I reached college, I was fitfully tired. That is to say, my soul was tired. I had already spent 15 years or so processing adult problems and advising a variety of people through life problems and decisions they should have been able to solve on their own. By that time, I had become the family mediator, confidant, a.k.a. "the nucleus" to all, and as such was left with nothing for myself.

I learned the hard way that there are consequences to giving of yourself without allowing yourself to also receive. This book is for the givers who give to the point of shivering in a corner with no clothes on because they gave that away too. This book is also for the takers. Takers, I hope you will see yourself in this narrative. I hope you will become keenly aware of how you affect those around you. This is therapy for me and for you all.

Secretly, I have always known an end would have to come for the ways we as humans are conditioned to sacrifice ourselves and our sanity. It is an unsustainable way of existing. I took a stab at coaching and even warned people and businesses all along my path. Unfortunately, we are far more responsive to chaos and suffering as a species than we are preventative, so we effectively destroy people to a point where well-being, self-care, and emotional/mental health must be prioritized.

The important piece to remember is that this is a journey. Life's a journey. While you may encounter angry, bitter moments in this book, you will also be reminded of what it means to grow on your own terms, while relishing in your success where you stand. My story is about perseverance, recognizing the directional signs in your life, finding your tribe, being a rebel elegantly and with a cause, self-love, and the true definition of "doing you."

NAMES AND DESTINY: MY STAMP OF APPROVAL

The archetype you are learning about in this book descended from the cosmos to planet Earth on March 27th, 1983. The stars aligned with both complexity and favor, adorning me with the leadership, passion, philosophical prowess, and adventurous spirit synonymous with the sign of Aries. I'm a proud ram: pioneering, dominated by Mars but with an earthly, ethereal, and nurturing nature I would later come into during one of the most challenging times in my life. For you astrology buffs and by western standards, I am an Aries sun, Virgo moon, Gemini rising, with a Venus right at home in Taurus. By sidereal/vedic standards, I am a Pisces sun, Leo Moon, Taurus Rising, with a Venus in Aries. I have had people debate me on which one is really powering this avatar, "Janine Nicole," but what I know is I feel the polarity of both of these realities. I embody both perspectives of the zodiac cycle. There is something about me that is dominant, yet soft. I am otherworldly spiritual with a heart that runs ablaze in love. I am organized, methodical, and even guarded, yet free-spirited and attached to nothing. I wax philosophical yet have a reverence for empirical evidence and intellect. I share all of this to say no one can tell you more about you, than you. They can illuminate pieces of the puzzle that lead you to deeper exploration, but ultimately you are the only judge and jury of who you are. You are not defined by what society says, your family, a love interest, or even those pesky ruminating thoughts that define you as a matter of a circumstance where you didn't show up as your best self. Our destiny isn't this elusive fairytale thing that esoteric types like me speak about to escape the practicality of life. Destiny is this journey we all must travel to fulfilling our missions here on Earth. How you reach your destination of transcending this human experience is both a matter of how you choose to play these hunger games and how much you allow yourself to surrender to what life wants to teach you.

You will hear me speak a bit about what I gleaned from an organization called the "Inheritance Project" during the beginning stages of the pandemic. I think we all spent our time sheltered-in-place in different ways. I'd like to think my time was spent cocooning, learning, and accepting the true essence of myself. Here's what I learned about my name at that time. To be really frank, my parents had no clue what they were naming me when they chose "Janine Nicole." I think they felt it was a good name to go through life with and were thankful some family members had some perspective on baby naming, so I didn't have to spend too many of my days Earthside unidentified. They didn't do what I did with my own children, combing through many websites and books on different names in search of a name that I felt the incoming soul could live with, thrive with, and fulfill the mission of that name. All the same, they did well. "Janine Nicole" has pizazz and timeless meaning.

At the height of my spiritual awakening, I felt drawn to investigate my name. I learned the following: Janine means "God's Gracious Gift," Nicole means "Victory of the People," and Dennis is the Welsh version of Dionysus, the Greek God of Bacchanalia, wine, and all things fruitful. When I realized this is what my last name stood for, it blew my mind. Those who love me know "bacchanalin" is my favorite word to use. We say nothing and do nothing by chance.

I operate from a place of reflection. I believe the people we encounter are mirrors and either reflect the light or the dark of human existence. That said, it has always been my mantra that it is not the leader's job to speak to their impact on others, but rather the job of those who are subject to their leadership. I am grateful to have had countless humans reflect the light back to me, the affirmation and confirmation that I have impacted them in positive ways. I'd like to think that notion is a gift, and that somehow, I am fulfilling my divine mission. As far as "Victory of the People," I have always had a deep understanding that my job here is to see that people are treated equitably and are provided with pathways to recognizing their own greatness. As a spiritual guide of mine has so eloquently said, I am a karma lord. Not that I intentionally or consciously govern karma, but that there is something about who I am that sets off a chain of events that restore balance and ensure justice is done.

If you haven't already decided that the synchronicity of my life is absurd, let me give you some more to chew on. My mom had always told us that "Dennis" was an Irish name and that we perhaps had some lineage from that region. After taking the Ancestry DNA test some years ago, I found out that she was onto something. We do have Irish lineage, but it doesn't stop there. You see, "Dennis," like many names given to African descendants, has been distorted to fit the anglophone perspective and sensibilities. As I shared earlier, the true name is not "Dennis," it is "Dionysus," which is Greek in origin. Dionysus was a god of fertility and all things bacchanalia, and wouldn't you know that some of our favorite food as a family is Greek and Bacchanalin... yeah, we are the pioneers of that. To say that the Dennis family is fertile is an understatement. I won't give you a headcount, but there are many of us, many generations deep, geographically spread out, and embodying a mosaic of cultures.

I remember as a child, my dad said that he had done some poking around in our history. In doing so, he found an ancestor of ours who fought in an Egyptian War. Fast forward to 2019, my youngest aunt on my mom's side visits Egypt. She brought me back a cartouche with my name on it. I felt this deep draw to decode the hieroglyphs to see if it really meant "Janine." The hieroglyphs came back as cobra, vulture, water, reed, water, feather in symbols. Egyptian hieroglyphs each have deep meaning on their own while symbolic. I learned that cartouches were used to represent the name and title of a monarch. They were written on tombs and coffins to mark which pharaoh was buried inside to help their souls find their way back to the body and move on to the next life. They were also worn as amulets to protect the pharaoh from evil spirits and bring good luck. Janine by Egyptian terms is a person of divine authority, sovereignty, royalty. Janine is connected to healing and restoration, a protector. Janine is a bearer of water, a shapeshifter of sorts who symbolizes transformation and understands we die and are born again many times over in life.

Dionysus in Egyptian times was syncretized to the God Osiris, lord of the underworld, the divine counterpart and brother to the Goddess Isis who also happens to have ties to my name Janine. While we just took a historical, otherworldly, and semi-deep dive into the many directions I have traveled in an effort to understand my name, the point is our names tell us much more of the story than we give them credit for. I have been an open vessel, eager to understand who I am and what my purpose is beyond the conventional attributions of career and socio-economic status. To me, life has always been bigger than what our naked eyes allow us to see and deeper than we allow ourselves to feel.

I know the universe dictates that I am both consequential

and inconsequential all at once. However, while in this body, it has made life a little more interesting understanding the people I may have been in other lifetimes and the bloodline I come from. On days where life feels icky, it's fun to remind myself that I am royalty and divine. Sounds absurd, but so are most other experiences we have while on this plane.

Evolving Soul Reflection: *I took you on a synchronistic and meaningful journey through my naming and how it has resulted in framing my destiny. So much of this journey is not about learning and being the smartest person in the room, but about remembering who we are at our core. Your job is to remember who and what you are. You are divinely designed to do something very specific here. Get excited about uncovering your true nature. Just as you patronize certain brands because their names have come to mean you will receive something useful or valuable, the same is true of the symbolism behind your name. Align with it. Celebrate it. Evolve with it.*

Let's have some fun. Look up the meaning of your name. Write it down below and reflect on what you think it means. How has your name shown up in your life? Is there any alignment between the meaning and history behind your name and who you have become to date? Conversely, if you never felt any connection to your name, what has your journey been with finding significance in your existence despite the name you were given?

Use the space below to document your evolving soul reflections.

THE ROOT WORK OF JANINE NICOLE

I was born in Flushing, Queens to Brenda and Anthony Dennis. Both of my parents are of West-Indian ancestry. My mom is Guyanese American and my dad native to Trinidad and Tobago. I feel like I have been a proud first-generation American my entire life. It's not that being purely American is chopped liver. It's just that being first-generation American colors your view of the world a certain way.

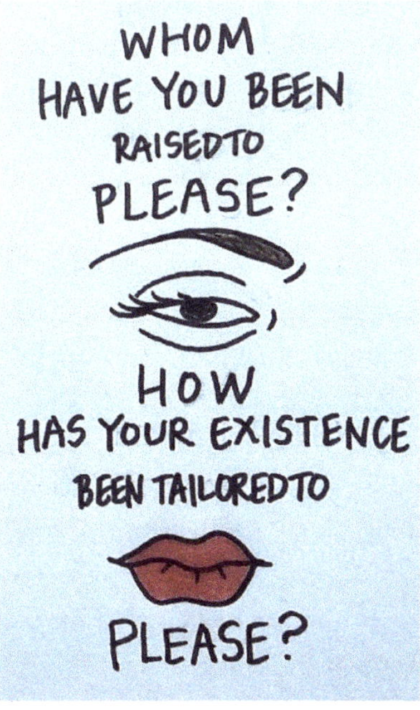

You certainly grow up with all the privileges of being American, but the struggle and beauty of life "back home" is indelibly etched in your mind and spirit for eternity. Your parents and grandparents would have it no other way.

There is both a spoken

and unspoken pressure that first-gen kids feel. It is especially felt if you are the oldest or the “mature one” of your crew. All the unrealized dreams, perceived successes, and folklore of better living in the States meant expected achievements. Add a healthy dose of generational trauma and a dedication to tradition and culture to that equation, and you have a unique way of growing up.

Early in life, I spent a lot of time with my grandparents on both sides, but more often my mom’s side of the family. They are the Guyanese side of the family. I call them the foundation setters and settlers. They have a very specific way in which they choose to see the world. For them, most things are either black or white, this or that. Education was above all else, and embracing the Guyanese culture was diluted down to the food we ate and the stories shared by my grandfather about Guyana. Speaking in Guyanese Patois was a no-no in my grandfather’s book. He wasn’t someone you questioned, but I wonder now if he thought this was the only way we would assimilate and be successful in this country. I need to believe that because for me there is no situation in which I am ever comfortable diluting anything about me to make others comfortable. That aside, this bunch are kind but strict. Each of them rose to various levels of success in their chosen careers. More notably, they each individually and collectively demonstrate a focus on being of service. This of all things they have impressed upon me resonates the most. This portion of the tribe is smart, purpose-driven, formulaic, and lives with a black and white lens of the world, and yet what lacked was love. It was noted early, but it would take at least two decades before I would fully understand the implications of this. We’ll come back to this theme later.

I have them to thank for consistently applauding and feeding my love of learning and curiosity for all things scholarly. One of the things I get a lot is that my level of professionalism is exemplary and that I am well spoken. I have my Guyanese crew to thank for this. They laid a foundation in me that made me into a disciplined professional and lifelong learner. I learned early on that living estranged from my partner-in-life for decades wasn't living or loyalty, but rather a robber of lifelong joy. This was how my grandparents lived for the better part of four decades by the way. No matter how much I found myself following their blueprint/formula throughout the years, I always secretly wondered if there could have been success and love and all the good and fun things on the other side of their monochromatic, formulaic life.

That is where my dad's side of the family comes in. Make room for deh Trinis. They are quite a bunch. If the sides of my family needed an illustration to describe it, yin and yang would be best. On this side, they are creative, loving, spiritual, and fun. These are my pleasure-seekers. There really was no particular formula any of my family members used for living their best lives on this side. They danced in their uniqueness and felt their way through life. Education was more rooted in life lessons than something you only get in a classroom. Love and duty to others lived here too. Paradoxically, so did greed, jealousy, and comparison. The combination of both these tribes ignited something different in me, and I liked it.

It was through my Trinidadian grandparents that I came to understand exactly how your life partnership should play out. My grandfather a.k.a. Papi loved my grandmother extraordinarily. They traveled. They laughed. They doted on each other and regarded one another like they were the best things in the universe. Now, their relationship was not without flaws. I found out some troubling things the older I became. Sidebar: It's funny how every year you get older comes with a new family secret. It's almost like a girl scout receiving her badges for demonstrating increasing levels of service. Nonetheless, these two answered my question for what was beyond the planning, perceived perfection, and lack of love. Good, bad, or indifferent, they lived life. While they always championed my discipline and accomplishments, they went out of their way to demonstrate love, connection, and the perfectly imperfect life. Still, the formula was a central theme for me. While I enjoyed their slackness, I questioned if more discipline and structure would have served this side. Especially where certain people (namely my father's siblings) proved to be callous, immature, disrespectful, and ungrateful throughout my life. This will undoubtedly be the final straw that will solidify for them why they have not much cared for me in the first place, but for me, this is freedom, my truth, and my voice putting words to the often-unspoken tales of families. No child really needs nor wants to carry the burden of hearing from their grandparents about the many ways their aunts and uncles had disappointed them, and yet I understand today that these details were shared with me because they knew I was the one to heal it all.

Ultimately, the disciplined side of the house felt like a warm blanket when the other side was exhibiting pure unadulterated bacchanal, and my pleasure-seekers were a refuge when the foundation-setters and settlers became asphyxiating and pompous. It was a ping pong effect for years. Remember my comment about how a new bone in the proverbial family closet gets revealed as you get older? The divide and the ping-pong effect diminished in time as I understood the complexities of each side. After a while, they all blended seamlessly on the canvas of my life, one color bleeding into the other. The truth I came to accept is that none of them was necessarily better or more impactful than the other. They have each tried hard to position themselves as being better, more sensible, and a bunch of other altruistic qualities. All I came to accept is that they were human. Within each of my family members lies an interesting paradox between the things they think they are and what they are embodying in life. Interestingly enough, I too have had to learn what I am and what I'm not. There were lessons galore with this bunch that informed how I would eventually design my own absurdly rebellious life.

Evolving Soul Reflection: *Your family members are humans on a journey, just like you. Give them grace and give yourself space to grow in a completely different direction that suits you and your life purpose. It is never mandatory to pass along toxicity, suffering, or hurt. You are designed to live life abundantly and blissfully. Take the best of what your roots, culture, and overall upbringing offered you in the form of lived and learned experiences and make it your own.*

I call this portion of the book "The Root Work of Janine Nicole" taken from the concept of the root chakra in the chakra system. The root of the chakra system focuses on our beginnings (some even believe that our experiences prior to our physical birth live here). The root chakra is represented by the color red and focuses on our stability, security, foundations and basic needs in a similar fashion to the bottom level in Maslow's hierarchy. We all have an inheritance of events, people, rituals, traditions that shape who we will become. Reflect upon your own upbringing and consider how it has shaped you. What do you want to carry with you and what are some attributes, traits, behaviors, ideologies, etc. that need to expire?

Use the space below to document your root work reflections.

THE TEMPLATES FOR LIFE

Each of us was given what I called a template for our lives. This template is primarily composed of the things your parents or guardians feel are necessary for your survival. The interesting thing is that the template is chock-full of ideologies, behaviors, traumas, cultural and ethnic intelligence, religious dogma, and political views, and very little of it has gone through a generational quality or sustainability check.

For the most part, we humans are wired to lean into comfort and conformity. Let's deal with conformity for a moment. According to a 2014 study conducted by Association for Psychological Science called "Children Conform to the Behavior of Peers; Other Great Apes Stick with What They Know," researchers Daniel B. M. Haun, Yvonne Rekers, and Michael Tomasello found conformity to be a unique human trait. Where each of the groups were noted as having "individually acquired behavior tendencies," in about fifty percent of instances where an alternative set of behaviors to their own was observed, the children of the study switched to the new, socially acceptable behaviors and/or strategy; whereas two great apes that were also studied almost never adjusted their behavior to the majority and instead stuck with what they knew.

This is important to consider as we examine the roles that comfort, conformity, and evolution play in informing each of our individual templates for life. There is a comfort in doing what has always been done and more importantly has appeared to work in the past for a significant number of people. By now, you have already started calculating what kind of family you came from; was it a group that was predisposed to taking risks, or is it a group that is a bit more conservative about how they show up in the world? For some of you yet, it may be a mixed bag of complexities that informs the template you are currently basing yourselves off.

The templates we are founded upon are not always inherently faulty, but what is troubling is how little and how late we start questioning the validity of the mold we are supposed to fit in to survive everything from family life to public life. In my case, I have always asked the bigger questions, but I didn't seriously task myself with understanding why I am who I am and what informed the evolution of Janine Nicole until my mid-thirties. It was at that time that I started unpacking the template I was handed, from the way I was taught to behave in professional spaces to how generational trauma was being perpetuated in both covert and overt ways.

I emptied 35 years' worth of societal norms, familial constructs, trauma, and my own unique experiences onto an empty table. It was my task to re-categorize everything in my life, creating a more refined template and overall construct for my life overall. The first step in that process was to uncover the truths in what I have been told. If any aspects of my mindsets were based on convenient lies, misinformation, or a lack of available information, I filled in the gaps accordingly and started creating new neural pathways for myself by subjecting myself only to what is based in fact.

From there, I started doing the nuanced dance of being disgusted by truth while also examining what I had learned from all my newly acquired knowledge and how it all made me feel.

Layering my wisdom with how I felt led me to learn what role intuition plays in guiding us through life. For the first time in my life, I was thinking way beyond what public school and higher education imparted on me. I even started rapidly transcending the lessons learned within my family as my rose-colored glasses were stepped upon, and I had to see the human in everyone who had informed my life up until that point. Every story begets another story, and every lie informs another lie. With a lot of frustration and anger, you wonder if you have been living an illusion your whole life and you question whether all the comfort and conformity was done to save you or if it was done to destroy the promise of who you might be if not held back by willful ignorance.

The truth is inconvenient and disruptive. It is, in fact, the antithesis of comfort and conformity. There is comfort when we all believe and agree upon a cascading cadre of mindsets and behaviors, but there is a danger, too. Individualization suffers where regression towards the lowest rung of human behavior is the norm. In this way, many in our global society will never know who or what they might have been had they been rebellious in the pursuit of the version of themselves that lies beyond the trusty template they were given at birth.

If nothing else, this book is a battle cry for expansion and evolution. I'm not saying throw out the templates you have been given (although some of you need to burn yours), but I am saying use this book as a guide to examine it more carefully to decide if it is helping you or hindering you.

> ***Rebel Elegance Reflection:*** *How we see ourselves inevitably determines how well we see others and treat them. In healthy work environments, we present ideas to our teams and ask them to refine the idea while it's in its infancy. Imagine how much further along we could be in our evolution as individuals and as a global*

family if we took the time to poke holes in the ways we live, the way we are governed, and how we think about things. Take a second to consider the magnitude of us collectively expanding in consciousness and awareness in an effort for all ideologies and behaviors to benefit the whole instead of an illusory majority that has yet to trust truth let alone themselves.

What is the composition of your template? How closely does your life today reflect the things you learned based on your culture, political, religious, and familial upbringing? What still feels obligatory for you and why?

Use the space below to document your rebel reflections.

PIDGIN
IS NOT WRONG

ACCENT
IS NOT BROKEN

SLANG
IS NOT UNEDUCATED

PATOIS
IS NOT IMPROPER

DECOLONIZE LANGUAGE

OUR LANGUAGE IS THE BEAUTY OF OUR SURVIVAL AND OUR TREASURE

THE GIFT OF OUR MOTHER TONGUE

As I shared previously, my maternal grandfather was very much against my brother and I learning and speaking Guyanese Patois. Speaking for myself, I had zero plans on following that directive. I listened intently to how they spoke and the cadence in which they spoke. It was my intention to not only learn it but perfect it. I thought it was strange that my aunts and uncles on that side had become this diluted version of who we were originally. If you have ever heard a Guyanese person or anyone from the Caribbean speak, it is like listening to a song of suffrage, survival, and refinement that tells the story of oppression and domination but dances in an unexpected sweetness of triumph and richness of culture. It was puzzling to me how anyone could want to abandon our dialect, our mother tongue.

Coming of age and going out to work illustrated exactly why my grandfather had reservations about us speaking in what he called "colloquial language." I learned that our society isn't kind to people who aren't White, Cisgender, Anglophone speaking people. If you don't speak the King's English, the assumption is that you are an ignorant person incapable of anything from higher-level cognition to intelligent discourse. My grandfather was trying to save us from being stigmatized along our journey. I never asked, but I presume along his career someone had pointed out his Guyanese accent, or someone who came to the U.S. before him warned of the perils of clinging too tightly to his mother tongue.

I did what I set out to do as a child eventually. I mastered both the Guyanese and Trini dialects. I even picked up some others along the way by virtue of having interactions with others from within the Caribbean diaspora. I love my culture and my ethnicity. When I started to consider the prospect of having kids, I knew I didn't want my culture to fizzle out with me. I wanted them to have the experience of hearing the beauty in our patois and the freedom in speaking it. My ancestors had to assume pseudo-white identities to assimilate and be accepted here. From the shores of Africa to the Caribbean and eventually to the U.S., the message both spoken and unspoken was you are a primitive people, a substandard collective; but never fear, White people are here to make you forget your essence. Part of that essence we all carry is how we speak. Imagine now for a second what it feels like for BIPOC (Black, Indigenous, People of Color) people to step outside of their homes daily knowing that they must become something other than themselves aesthetically and linguistically to have relevance. Personally, I have code-switched my entire life. I never realized how exhausting it was until I encountered others like myself in the workforce allowing for a small crevice of freedom for me to speak as I am accustomed. My usual is a mix of the proper English I was taught, my Caribbean patois, and slang.

I want to address the role of slang a.k.a. colloquial language. Black people have been trying to reclaim their sovereignty since before they kinda sorta let us loose from the plantations. Every land we have been displaced from, every slave journey, and every year we have spent trying to survive on this rotating rock, required us to be innovative in how we communicated with one another day-to-day, from one human atrocity to the next, and yet in other times provided us with words we could relax into among our kin where we were being consistently erased. Slang, or as it was once called "Ebonics," was never the issue. The issue is that white people couldn't access it, but that was only for a time, because one thing we do know about white people is they will not be left behind.

In time, they appropriated and made sure to commodify our latest invention of linguistics, but this time for profit. I cringe to recall the many times I had to endure white men and women using slang in a corporate environment in all their fragile yet privileged glory. There I was expected to rise to their monochromatic expectations, speaking a language that is not my own, one that they have never taken the care to perfect, and that is quite frankly a poor standard for human expression. American English is quite literally the squalor of language, but we expect people who emigrate to the U.S. to speak it as if it is a prize. The prize is in direct correlation to socioeconomic status, but even with the achievement of greater social status, many of our superiorly articulate brethren have been reminded that no amount of education, anglophonic prowess, or etiquette will ever make us more human in the eyes of a white person.

We must be honest with ourselves that we have been lied to, bamboozled, led astray as our Ascended Master, Malcolm X, once said. Everything you have come to believe about what constitutes intelligence to what makes for professional behavior is a lie. From the time that someone has to change any aspect of themselves to live a decent life, the cost is too pricey, and you are in effect eroding their being.

I speak in Guyanese and Trini Patois and any other African descended and influenced manner I choose because it is my birthright to do so, and it is a cosmic nod to the ancestors that there is still a promise of freedom in the expression of our languages that their descendants are actively working towards.

> **Rebel Elegance Reflection:** *Language is a key component of our identities. My story is unique in a sense, but likely akin to so many others who have been ostracized or felt like they were being discounted because English wasn't their first language or because the way they speak isn't seen as professional enough, so they play out a few different personas to appease the tastes of white people. We must stop doing this to one another under the guise of professionalism. You can't preach diversity, equity, inclusion, and belonging and disparage someone for the ways they choose to express themselves. This is colonizer behavior created by white people and often perpetuated by people of color against their own to seem like they are conformists and team players. Reality check: you are just doing ages-old dirty work for white folx; you're a mascot and pawn. Time to wake up!*
>
> *How has language impacted your life? What assumptions do you make about someone because of their mother tongues? How might you shift the way you choose to express yourself through language to engender more of your personal identity and freedom?*

Use the space below to document your rebel reflections.

AIN'T NO HALF STEPPIN'

My family did not sacrifice to come here from the West Indies for me to play small. This is the thing I tell myself when I am ready to shrink or throw in the towel. It made me proud anytime one of my grandparents got excited about my accomplishments. There was always a little spark of happiness in their eyes and faces (especially my grandmothers) that let me know I had done something important for our family's legacy. My Grandma Wills would always say, "Yes gyurl, you keep going and get everything you want. Let people think whatever they want. God will always provide." My Grandma Marie would say in her beautifully charismatic Trini patois, "Go gyal! Doh let anyone stand in your way. Yuh doing deh ting. I'm so proud of you." I do what I do for me. I do it for my kids, but more importantly I do it for them in the physical and with them in the spiritual realms as they have never left my side despite them no longer being here. I wish they were all here now for me to call and celebrate with. I wish I could speak like we used to so they can see that I have come into full understanding of all the clues they left for me.

I suppose those wants are a matter of my human sensibilities getting the best of me. The reality and truth is they are perpetually here with me. I honor them daily via my ofrenda, ancestral altar. They are around me and within me. There ain't no half steppin'. I say that with some defiance as colloquial language was blasphemous in their eyes. As daunting as it is to carry the weight of my family, I know my grandparents have passed the baton to me to continue progressing our bloodline in my own absurd, rebellious, and purposeful way.

"Freeing Ourselves"

Don't think it isn't lost on me that my words, my truths, will anger some people. The thing about our lived experiences is we are allowed to call them as we see them. It has to be wildly uncomfortable to have to confront yourself for the first time through the very public words of another, detailing the ways in which you have harmed them over time. I share what has occurred in my life not to put the cast of characters on blast or even to place blame, but rather to free myself from having to be silent to preserve their ego and feelings, which are two things I am not ever responsible for. I share my challenges in life because somewhere out there is a young man or a teenage girl or even a middle-aged woman coming to grips with all they have endured in life and suffering in isolation unbeknownst to anyone from the grip fear has had on them should they consider lifting their voices. By being ourselves and living out the absurdity of this life, we empower other humans to do the same.

Here's what gets deeply problematic for most people when someone like me starts to speak out openly and honestly. The truth is sometimes messy. I have discovered through the years that people are much more at home with lies and falsehoods than they are with the hardcore truths of our more pressing matters. We have become a species of convenience. It is evidenced in how we participate in the world and most unfortunately in how we operate with one another. The truth often is far from being convenient, which is why dishonesty is rampant. Let's take "infidelity" for instance. It is far easier for some people to start and maintain an outside relationship to fulfill an unmet need than for them to address the issue at home. In reality, the options are clear. Be open and honest with your partner about your dissatisfaction, which could lead to changed behavior, therapy which facilitates changed behavior, or you decide to end it all. There is clarity in those choices, but the incidents of infidelity remain a consistent occurrence in our society.

We get angry when we have been lied to by others, yet we bypass the ways in which we betray ourselves by telling ourselves lies about everything from what work we would be happier doing to who we truly love. Lying isn't wrong merely because religious dogma and ethics tell you so. It is wrong because it betrays your heart and causes unnecessary suffering for everyone involved.

In what ways have you lied about who you are and what you desire in life? What was the breaking point where you couldn't betray your heart any longer?

Use the space below to document your evolving soul reflections.

DO THIS, NOT THAT

For a long time, I lived by the formula. There was always an individual flame that would come out to play once in a while, but ultimately, I grew up believing there was a "way" you did this thing called life. By formula I mean, go to school, do well in school, focus on your studies, find a vocation, be thankful for that vocation, don't make waves, rise, and show up in life accordingly. This, my friend, is what we call first-generation problems and perfectionism. These two things are passed on to everyone in a certain way, but with first-generation kids, these themes are far more palpable and prominent. The message and social and cultural cues we receive say life is meant to be a continuous climb to prestige and status via relinquishing how you feel and what makes you glow from the inside out as an individual. Work hard. Life is hard. Be the best. Forget the rest. More formulas.

While this all sounds good and makes for a solid foundation for any child, it is utterly boring and lacks the inspiration. I have learned to color outside of the lines of what is defined as a normal life. What is a life without knowing yourself, becoming who you are meant to be, and expressing it boldly, rebelliously even? It is no life at all.

I eventually learned that seeing things in "black and white" and living life by perceived formulas, and/or culturally prescribed notions of success do not always result in success, but I was a meek, mild child and a firstborn, so I aimed to please everyone, never knowing that this very act would undermine one important person. That person was me.

If you ever pay attention to the rebels and/or misfits of society, there is a certain freedom they come to enjoy. While everyone sits around judging their every move, they are busy living life on their own terms. They may be stumbling every step of the way, but the point is they are living life their way. The people who judge their path do so for two reasons: 1) They are in danger of harming themselves or others which is valid, or 2) They secretly wish they had enough courage to live hedonistic lives that are tethered to desire and passion rather than rules and convention.

I was always an outlier. I never dressed like my peers, so I got made fun of. I didn't think like most. Unlike today's kids, "eccentricity" was not a welcomed attribute in "The View" where I grew up. In the '90s, there wasn't exactly a safe space for Black girls who happened to be wicked smart, mouthy, or could recite hip hop lyrics as if entering a cipher as quickly as a Fiona Apple song. There was no space held for girls like me who already knew what they wanted out of life; the ones who could craft science experiments in their sleep and write like a scholar, but would destroy boys in Mortal Kombat and talk comic books. I was different. I was layered, cerebral, and dare I say otherworldly where others were striving to be one thing to be liked. Popularity and I had a wayward relationship then. I didn't give too many fucks about who liked me as long as they kept it to themselves, but they never could. The whispers as I would pass certain cliques, eye rolls, and people getting in my face because they assumed I was the nice, smart girl was when I started to learn where the shadow/dark parts of me lived.

To this day, I credit my grit and edge in business and life

to childhood bullying. I hated it at the time, but had I not developed my street smarts then, I may have been even more unequipped to manage the many difficult and insidious circumstances I encountered over the course of my personal and professional life.

As I mentioned earlier, you will repeat life lessons until you master them, so in hindsight it is no shock to me that I met an entirely new group of bullies when I went into the world of work. My 20s brought me some old school lessons with a futuristic beat.

My first job out of school at Aerotek wasn't my first choice as a job. My hope was to join NYU Medical Center after completing a successful internship with them, but alas, they had no openings for me. Aerotek seemed like the right fit for my background, and it allowed me to move out of my childhood home finally.

As I think back, my intuition had been trying to warn me of the perilous waters of life since I was a child. Had I trusted it and myself more I probably could have avoided many challenges or at a minimum been better at anticipating them.

> ***Rebel Elegance Reflection:*** *Always be ready to reflect upon how you show up in the world, but also remember that every person's emotions or reactions are not your baggage to carry. Your job is to be courageous every day in being the best version of you possible. The people you encounter will project and spew their opinions, insecurities, misinformation, and (as I like to say) bad juju on you because they need healing and reflection. Extend them love, grace, and space, and carry on, rebel.*
>
> *Time to do some reflecting, rebels. What have you identified as some of your more challenging behaviors and attributes? How have these aspects helped or harmed you throughout life? Part of becoming better*

versions of yourself is being able to give yourself grace and kindness. How can you begin to acknowledge and love those aspects of yourself more?

Use the space below to document your rebel excellence reflections.

"THE VIEW"

In 1987, we moved from Jamaica Hills, NY to a town in Long Island called Lakeview. It's a small town within West Hempstead, New York. It was a good place to grow up. Most notably, it's where I developed my grit and strength. Conversely, it is a place wrought with both good and bad memories of people and situations that shaped me for life.

This little town of Lakeview was a middle-class neighborhood. Everyone knew everyone. Even if you didn't know a person's name, you knew their face. I'd like to think more people knew my face than my name, but interactions with people from there in recent years suggests I am misguided in my assumption. That is to say, there are always more people tuned into you than you care to recognize.

I learned early on that being different and/or disciplined are not only traits few people have, but they also play into people's insecurities and fears. I have been unlocking Pandora's box of fears and insecurities my whole life just by being comfortable being me. I never knew why I was the chosen mark for girls in school to bully and test. From the one girl who took my She-Ra metal lunch box and hit me in my face in elementary school to the myriad of girls who attempted to jump me for shits, giggles, and street cred, it was always a mystery why this place my parents moved me to for a better life was wrought with so much turmoil. There is no question that I arrived in Lakeview as an innocent little girl who loved Jem and the Holograms, and all things rainbows and bright, but exited a young woman who would cut you if you breathed wrong near her. One of my more notable bully encounters took place when I was in 7th grade. I went out for a state pageant called Miss Junior America. I was an aspiring model and passionate dancer back then. To enter the pageant, I had to get businesses in the neighborhood to sponsor me. Our family accountant at the time was instrumental in garnering me the necessary support, and it was from there that those flyers with my face on them started going up in local establishments. The pageant was in the Summer of '96. I didn't win, but I came in 3rd runner up. This was huge because I was the only Black girl in the lineup of winners in a very monochromatic competition. By the time I returned to school for my 7th grade year, the goons were ready to go. In this bully encounter, I was advised from that morning that a certain girl was going to jump me. Imagine the lack of focus you have for schoolwork when you need to prepare for war after school. I had my friend Dee-Dee braid my hair during 7th period and hold my jewelry. From the time I left school, it was a movie. The whole school was walking home with a sense of anticipation and excitement that you would expect before a Mike Tyson brawl. Words were exchanged as soon as we were officially off school property. Her battle rap to start the feud was, "I heard you have something to say to me," and the fighting began. Some older dudes pulled us apart, and she distinctly said, "I don't care if you are Miss Junior America, I will cut you!" It was at that moment that something snapped in my head. All I remember thinking is "I will cut you before you cut me." I envisioned getting home to get a butcher knife off my mom's butcher block. I did just that. I walked briskly, unlocked the front door, and went straight for the knife to go handle her. Thankfully, there were friends and responsible neighbors I now regard as "earth angels" who urged me against the act and reminded me of who I was. I never chopped her up as intended, but it marked a day and time where I met my shadow for the first time. I wasn't a violent person, but one too many bullies unearthed an archetype of "Janine Nicole" that they never expected and one that I didn't know was there. It was scary. I was a child not equipped with any advice on how to channel dark feelings. The strength cultivated in Lakeview, better known as "The View," served me well as I became a young woman working in Corporate Amerikkka. No, I didn't pull knives on anyone beyond that point, but in a metaphorical way I learned to keep myself armed and ready to draw my weapon when needed.

For a long time, I was unclear as to why I kept having the same issues with bosses I reported to in my jobs. I often wondered why the narratives among so-called friends and family were similar. All these instances were a mystery until I realized I was the common denominator. Essentially, it was something about me that consistently rubbed people the wrong way. While I could have spent my days oblivious to the synchronicity of all of these events, I chose to peel back the layers in an effort to discover who I was and how I have impacted the people around me.

You may be wondering if I have figured it all out. The simple answer is: Yes and No. I would be misleading you to position my journey as though it has been dutifully resolved. What I have come to realize is the universe will deliver you people and circumstances until you learn the lesson. In every way, I can attest that I have reached a point of self-awareness and confidence across the board. Life is an amalgamation of trials, errors, and lessons. For as long as we live, none of life's questions are fully resolved, but we instead strive for improved understanding. It is through that lens that we can begin to make better decisions; live more purposefully and in effect become better human beings for it.

Purposeful Human Reflection: *Being a "purposeful human" is about acknowledging and accepting that you have a unique mission and purpose to execute above and beyond the usual focus of day-to-day life. The second prong is trusting yourself to follow your divine path bravely and in full recognition that it is just one rung of an incredible climb. Where there is purpose, there is an elevated perspective and dedication to the divine plan that lies well beyond conventional understanding of our individual contributions to humanity.*

My hometown of Lakeview wasn't just "The View"; it changed my view on the world and myself. What does it mean to you to be a "purposeful human"? Reflect on one or two defining moments you have had in your life that changed the way you saw yourself. Did that change lead you closer to finding your purpose or further from it?

Use the space below to document your purposeful human reflections.

MODEL BEHAVIOR

January 24th, 2004

I'm proud of my modeling career. I've been working diligently at it since 2001 at this point, but I made a lot of headway in 2003. I not only became a spokesmodel for a clothing line, but I was featured as "Aspiring Model of the Month" for June 2003 on the Urban Upscale website. In addition to that, I did a shoot for a freelance photographer in July and subsequently got signed by Stars Models after attending a casting call for Sex and the City in August. So yeah... this modeling thing is working out. I hope to be doing more big things this year as well as putting out my modeling website, shooting a portfolio, and creating my own clothing line.

May 17th, 2004

As far as my modeling career goes, it has been phenomenal. I did a morning television show for CBS in April called "Living it up with Ali and Jack." I was a featured model for a tooth whitening segment. I was also named Crunk Beauty of the Month for May 2004 and listed as "Beautiful" on the BlackCuties.com website. I'm now listed with SoloModels.com and presently being considered for a reality television show and two magazines. I'm extremely proud of myself and I will continue to push myself in this industry.

For as long as I can remember, I have been drawn to the arts and entertainment. I was majorly into music, dance, and modeling growing up. From Elementary School through Junior High School, I took everything from Ballet to studying Hip-Hop under the direction of an MTV dancer back in the day. I was exposed to Alvin Ailey and Kenny G at an early age. Kenny G was my inspiration for choosing the Saxophone in Junior High. He played a Soprano Saxophone which wasn't available, so I took the next best option, the Alto Sax. I went on to receive top honors in Band, but also played in Jazz Band placing in NYSSMA and All County Competitions in NY.

Modeling was an ongoing thing for me. I shared a bit about vying for the title of Miss Junior America in 1995. I didn't win, but I placed 3rd runner up. Prior to that, my mom and I did runway shows in Harlem with Vanputten Productions for quite a few years back in the day.

There is something that comes alive in me when I'm in front of the camera. I have also always been partial to a quality thread, having had a grandmother who was an extraordinary seamstress and who would sew me the most gorgeous dresses and costumes as a child. For me, fashion was my way of expressing myself without uttering a single word. I went my own unique and eccentric way when it came to my style; some of it was scoffed at because it didn't mirror the vibe of the day. I never let that deter me from making the fashion statement I desired. I came up in the time of logo t-shirts with the name brand splattered across the chest, jeans and Jordans with the Jansport bookbag that could barely hold a single book. Pretty much every girl in my high school dressed this way. To me, it was a bore and unoriginal, so I wore what I liked and learned to take the criticism on the chin like a champ.

When I left high school, I dove headfirst into taking modeling and dancing more seriously. My dad would always speak about the number of times he had to chauffeur me to casting calls in the city. The more interesting story, however, is what I encountered while taking this journey as an aspiring model.

We're talking the early 2000s in modeling here. We had yet to elevate our consciousness to the point of the current body positive movement. I was in my late teens and much tinier in stature at that time. For anyone who has been in this industry for a time they will tell you that it will either build your character or break you. Imagine for a second walking into a casting call for a gig with your comp card in tow and having a casting director look at you and just say "next!". It feels like a gut punch. I had casting directors who asked me if I would ever consider getting my nose done. I had another gentleman who owned a clothing line ask me if I would consider closing the gap in my teeth. He never made a name for himself with that brand, but consider how that lies with a young adult who truly wants to make it in the modeling industry being met with those requests. It wears on you, and if you're not careful they will have you out there looking like a caricature of yourself.

In one instance, I went to a casting call for a runway production. They were accepting young women of average height, so 5′5″ to 5′8″. That was revolutionary for the time. When I showed up and got up to the casting table, they said, "You're beautiful, but you may be best suited for commercial modeling. Your proportions are bigger than what most runway productions will accept." I was a size 2. There is something gravely wrong with an industry that believes a woman that is a size 2 is too large to walk a runway. The women that I would see getting the approving smirks looked like corpses quite frankly. It was the first time I was confronted with the concept of body image and how the media and entertainment industries were culpable in creating pervasive distortions in what constitutes beauty in our society.

I won't lie to you, there were brief moments in time when

I found myself tuning into plastic surgeons and medi-spa places more than I ever would have if not for the modeling industry. I had neither the means to make any changes to myself nor a true desire, but they definitely had me investigating for a time there. Ultimately, I decided that any outlet that couldn't accept me as-is with no modification was not a place I needed to be.

Let's shift gears a bit and revisit my time auditioning for music videos. As I mentioned, dancing for me was a lifelong pursuit that continued on long after I gave up on the music industry's ability to treat women with respect and not as sex slaves. Again, this is the early 2000s, so we're talking about the era of the Video Vixen. Every artist from Usher to Ludacris made damn sure to have copious amounts of eye candy in their videos to draw attention to the music. If you remember that era, there was a look and there was a small rotation of video vixens getting the bulk of the work, largely for their "exotic" looks. There was even an agency back then called Ethnicity Models that had signed most of the notable video vixens of the time. When you read the individual model profiles, it would list them with their ethnicities as if you were reading some sort of scientific or anthropological abstract on a species. It was acceptable at that time, but by today's standards that sort of objectification and colorism would be rejected.

I didn't exactly want to just be eye candy; I knew I had this background in dance and had every capability of being in the spotlight not only for my beauty but for my skill. So, I went out to casting calls for music videos, aiming at ones I felt would allow me to display my dancing prowess. I won't name names of the acts I auditioned for, because it doesn't much matter who they are, and also, I won't let the fixation of their names detract your attention from the point of the story. There are two casting calls that were defining for me. One of them was for a well-known rapper who liked me enough that I made it to the final audition. Upon offering to cast me in the video for which I was literally screaming on the inside, he says to me, "You should give me your number and come chill sometime. There's a lot more work to get with us." The second notable instance was for another video where the director flat out told me he was casting for a video for Alicia Keys and Musiq Soulchild and that if I wanted to ensure I would be casted for these opportunities, I should come out to the club with him and his friend with one of my friends so we could "get to know each other better." I have been told to come to the studio and "chill" and then we can go shopping for whatever you like by another well-known rapper disappointingly of Trini descent.

Keep in mind, I was in college completing my undergraduate degree. Most of the young women who were auditioning saw modeling and dancing as their sole paths. These subtle to blatant asks of me giving my time and clearly sleeping with people in the industry to get ahead were disappointing nudges that my desire to be a model and dancer in these ways was not my path. It made me sick to my stomach to think of having drinks with these men let alone sleeping with them for a gig. It called into question the integrity of the entire industry.

By 2005, I had decided to leave modeling and dancing behind me and focus on a career that celebrated my intellect and allowed me to climb the proverbial ladder in a more ethical and moral manner. I have always missed it just a bit. Beyond 2005, I found ways to stay connected to dance by taking classes in Jazz and learning Belly Dance, which allowed me to go on to perform quite a bit before I had my firstborn.

I had always wondered if the industry would change and if certain dark aspects of it would be acknowledged aloud. When the stories of Harvey Weinstein and even Jeffrey Epstein broke, among others, I knew the day of reckoning for the entertainment industry was afoot. I wasn't shocked in the least, but rather relieved to see women speaking out about the disgusting underpinnings of Hollywood. The entertainment industry is founded upon perverse dealings and dare I say dark energy. I'm not saying everyone in it is on that vibe, but it's not hard to tell who has sold their soul and who is doing their very best to maintain their dignity and value system while sharing their gifts with the world. Equally so, I have been elated to see a more body positive movement take flight in the modeling space. Gone are the days where we praise the model that is seemingly wasting away in her own body. As a woman who is now a size 8 many moons past childbearing and not interested in the least to ever be a size 2 again, I value brands that represent what the everyday woman looks like. I'm here for the movement of women to be praised for every stretch mark, stomach roll, curve, and imperfection. I'm in no way aiming to shame women who are skinny naturally. I am however, suggesting that we desperately need a new narrative for what is healthy and, more importantly, beautiful. It was a long time coming. I don't regret my time as a model and dancer. It forced me to love myself fiercely as I am. It was my test in self-love. I'd like to think I've passed with flying colors.

> ***Purposeful Human Reflection:*** *There are defining moments in each of our lives where we will be confronted with questions of our value system and even tasked with defending it. Sometimes your dreams are not meant to be a forever thing, but rather a moment in time to fortify who you will become. Sure, there are many pitfalls to the way I was handled as a model and a dancer, but look at what I learned about myself, about self-love, about being a woman with integrity. Being purposeful means being willing to acknowledge when you are on a path that is out of alignment with who you are as a person. Purpose requires knowledge of self and a lot of courage to do what is best for you even if it means leaving something you love and want behind.*
>
> *Push through, purposeful humans! Think about*

your value system and when you have felt challenged to uphold your values. What was that instance? Did you have to let go of something or someone you truly wanted?

Use the space below to document your purposeful human reflections.

CORPORATE AMERIKKKA: THE HOUSE OF CARDS

As I mentioned previously, my growing up in "The View" undoubtedly colored my view of the world and the nature of people. I started my journey as a working person on March 27th, 1997, when I turned 14. I did not wait one day past my 14th birthday to get my working papers. Unfortunately, at that time, more employers were turning kids away at 14 because hiring at that age had not worked out well for them. I had the good fortune of having a friend of the family connect me with a job working as a waitress for a Jewish Temple that doubled as a catering hall. I knew that if they gave me the chance to interview, I could get the job because I knew how to sell myself. Fortunately, they gave me the opportunity and true to form I got the job. I did that job for a few years followed by a slew of responsible jobs in retail through my high school years.

Up until my college years, I had bosses and experiences that built my character rather than tried to break it. That all ended once I graduated in 2005. It was then that I moved from the comfortable to the uncomfortable. My first job out of school was for Aerotek in their Scientific Group. In hindsight, staffing wasn't the dream, but I saw it as a gateway into Corporate HR. That I was able to capitalize on my science background while jumping into my career made it a worthwhile endeavor. Their process back then required you to meet with key team members for dinner to build rapport. I understood the purpose, but the introvert in me was leery. After many calls and dinners with the team, I was hired and started working for the company in July 2005. Fairly quickly thereafter, I was thrust into an environment of mostly newly graduated college students who were given responsible roles for having the gift of gab but who lacked in decorum and integrity. For the first time in my career, I was paired up with a mentor who was the only Black woman in Engineering at the time. It was the first time I had to be faced with my otherness in Corporate Amerikkka. In time, she became more than my mentor; we became friends, sharing similar yet different struggles of being the only Black women in our divisions trying to do valuable work on teams that were often not aligned with our values.

I spent about nine months at Aerotek. Part of my time was spent working in Manhattan, doing the city commute from Suffolk, Long Island, into the mean streets of NYC daily. My rotation was hustling to the train at 5:41am, work by 7:30am, run like hell to catch the 6:21pm train home, gym, liquor store for wine, cook dinner while watching Law & Order, and go to sleep by 9pm. It was far from a Mary Tyler Moore experience or even Sex and the City episode. There was little that was sexy about this job. Unless, of course, we count the fact that there was a bit of a harem going on within my team that exposed me for the first time to what sexual harassment in the workplace looks like. There was this guy, let's call him "Mr. Casanova," who was the lead on Scientific at the time. He was also a married man with a child, so he was considerably older than most of us on the team. The team in the NYC office comprised three women, including myself, and three men. Mr.

Casanova was dating one of the women on my team and more than that would passive-aggressively let me know that I needed to "open up" to them. He was consistent in his flirting and quite frankly a grade A asshole. You know the type, thought he was god's gift to women, could rattle off the firms he'd worked for with a sort of snobbery, parasitic in demeanor and nature. The whole damn team except for two others was toxic; I know that now. If they felt you weren't falling in line with their shenanigans and foolishness, they had a rule that a team member could pull you into a meeting to discuss how they felt so it could be rectified. Those meetings were far from empathetic and felt more like bullying. Mr. Casanova pulled me in once and that was the last time I tolerated that. In December of 2005, we had our company holiday party at this pub in Times Square. I was very much against attending as I saw these people more than I saw my then boyfriend and my family at this point, plus I just didn't like them very much; they were messy in ways my 22-year-old mind had yet to understand. I went because the few women of color in the office had decided to go for a bit to "show face" for an hour and then leave to go hang the way we preferred to. So, I went and one of the first people I met was Mr. Casanova, smug, aptly intoxicated, and sizing me up. I said hello, and he bent down and whispered in my ear, "You look good. I'm glad you came out." I thanked him and moved on to speak with others. That night, I met him again, he mentioned that the job was crap, and he may be moving on. I agreed and we conversed a bit. At the end of the conversation, he says to me, "You know, Janine, you're actually cool. I've been trying to get your attention, but you are not easy. You and I should hang out sometime and get to know each other." Got em! I never called, and I ensured I properly distanced myself from him going forward. He eventually left the company and that was the end of him. His "girlfriend" on the team however, continued to rise to prominence partly on skill but mostly on her southern charm. A bit of a loose cannon herself and about six months into my time with them, she randomly hauls off and swats my behind one day at the office. In full disclosure, I wanted to choke her, but professionalism. Instead, I escalated the event up the ranks to the Director of Staffing who hired me. Needless to say, the investigation rotation was wrought with issues. A resolution was never brought to my attention, nor was there an atonement for what I had to endure. Let us be clear about something here. Black people, people of African descent, don't appreciate nor enjoy some of the shenanigans that Corporate Amerikkka has exposed us to. I'm not saying that people of color don't sexually harass in the workplace too. I'm suggesting that Corporate Amerikkka is quite visibly a white man's game, and it wasn't designed with us "others" in mind. What ends up happening in time is we, in my case Black Women, end up retarding our values to survive work environments steeped in discrimination, harassment, and the consistent erosion of our sovereignty. In this situation, my agency over my body was taken from me. Speaking up for myself was automatically tabled as me being difficult and hard to work with, which in turn looked like an opportunity for white men and women to take a corrective stance with me, as perhaps their ancestors would have on the plantation. I was bold back then, but not bold enough. I still cared too much about the white standard of professionalism.

On my last day with Aerotek, my boss a.k.a. Mr. Needle called me up at my Long Island office in a rage for why I hadn't gone to a specific client site. I kindly let him know that it was my last day, and I was cleaning up things to depart. He said, "So, you decided on your own not to go?" I said, "Yes, I did." He told me, "Leave now!" I quietly said, "No problem." As I hung up, one of the other supervisor's phones rang and I knew he was being instructed to do something pertaining to me. That supervisor hung up and came over to me sheepishly to say that he needed to see my bags and my desks to ensure that

I wasn't taking anything. He asked me to close my computer and promptly leave. It's worth noting that this was not done behind closed doors. I was addressed in this manner, as if a criminal, in a cubicle environment where everyone could hear what was being said. I turned to that supervisor and told him that if he didn't get away from me, I would throw the laptop through the window. He backed up. I packed up, flung my pocketbook over my shoulder, and walked out with my head high. The day was sunny and warm. I already had my new gig, and I was headed to my dad's house just around the corner for some tea with my Grandma Marie and good Trini food. What I can tell you with certainty, and this cannot be debated, is I was not insubordinate. I was not a difficult person. I was a young Black professional who was wise beyond her time and had a work ethic and integrity that didn't align with that experience. I learned then that speaking your mind was only for white people. Mediocrity and being unprofessional was only allowed if you were white. That I dared to be anything different than what the system wanted me to be got me labeled in ways that were unwarranted and inaccurate. This would not be the last time I encountered this double standard in my career.

> ***Purposeful Human Reflection:*** *Every job you have will teach you something about yourself and others. Your career is supposed to be rewarding in the ways that are most meaningful to you. It should make you evolve, build your character, allow you to acquire new knowledge, skills, and abilities. Work should never erode who you are. You deserve to feel safe at the one place we all spend more time than at home. There is absolutely nothing more soul draining than waking up at the crack of dawn to report to a job that devalues you as a person. Choose yourself every time. Speak up, be heard, take up space, contribute meaningfully, and*

when it seems like it is all going to shit... know when it is time to go.

Time to do some reflecting, purposeful humans. Think about how you want to feel while doing work that you enjoy. What would you need from that corporate environment to feel whole and respected? How aligned are your values with the work you are doing today? Part of being successful professionally is predicated on how you choose to define success for yourself. How can you begin to define success in healthy and practical ways?

Use the space below to document your purposeful human reflections.

“THE MINSTREL SHOW”

According to Brittanica.com the minstrel show is “an American theatrical form popular from the early 19th through the early 20th centuries founded on the premise of comical reenactments of racial stereotypes.” This definition alone is absurd. As my one course in African American Studies in undergrad illustrated, there was nothing comical about those shows except for the White devils entertained by it. Black face exaggerated and caricature-like lips, bright eyes to look alive and put on the appearances that they were happy about the performance was the plight of the minstrel. Like most things in our sordid history here in the States, that foolery didn’t stop in the early 20th century. In fact, it took a quantum leap to 2005 when I worked for Aerotek. There were many things that were offbeat with my onboarding to that job, but the one that sticks out for me was this bit about having to do a dance once you place your first person at a client. From the time I heard of this tradition, I was turned off. I put this dance off for as long as I could. I imagine that this was something they felt lightened the mood and created some sort of camaraderie, but for me it was a nightmare, as I was more of the kind to want to do my work and stay out of the circus antics. It also helps to understand that neglecting this mandate was impossible and made me out to be "difficult," "not a team-player," "guarded." The actuality of things was that I was and still am an introvert. I am also a first generation American. We were taught very much to the demise of our own success in Corporate Amerikkka that we go to work to work and get the job done. There was no discussion of how to navigate the interpersonal realities of the Corporate World. The little that was shared with me was that I should not get too involved or friendly with people as it breeds trouble. It wasn't until I started experiencing pushback for how I showed up at work, that I confided in one of my aunts who had worked for EY and other major firms telling me that interpersonal skills are almost more important than how well you do your job. She was right. Whether it was Aerotek or every subsequent company I was with, it was clear those that got ahead had the gift of gab and would go to any extent to appear to be personable.

Back to this dance, one fateful morning I was running to catch the E train as usual. A very kind woman pulled me aside gently and let me know I had split my skirt. How embarrassing! She was a friggin' angel for that. I ended up being late to work that day. I had to go back up to 34th Street and walk over to Manhattan Mall with my blazer tied to cover my exposed bum, awaiting the opening of Express so I could buy some slacks. When I eventually got to work, I was the laughingstock of my group as they were all aware of my little mishap. I took that like a champ. That same morning, I was due to debut this dance. The anxiety I felt as well as annoyance was more than I needed that day. Nonetheless and very much in line with how Black people show up at work, I did what needed to be done. They rang that dumb ass gong as if I was on Showtime at the Apollo and I said, "in the spirit of what I had to do to get here today, I am going to do the running man." I busted out my best running man to the cheers and laughter of a sea of White faces. After I stopped, I was met with a barrage of "that was so awesome" and high fives. Again, all White people. I was the only Black woman on my team and in the office that day. In total, there were only four of us and one Latina. It occurred to me that they had reduced me to a minstrel show. Yes, everyone had to do it regardless of race, but there was no lens for cultural sensitivity or even neurodiversity. It helps to understand that they also felt at the time they were cutting edge by offering diversity training that was just as riddled with cultural insensitivity and racism as their asinine gong dance.

I've never forgotten this experience. It is the very reason I named this chapter "Corporate Amerikkka: The House of Cards." Ultimately, we have a workforce that is founded on practices that were handed down from the plantation, carried on through segregation, and then again through the Civil Rights Era to what is now allegedly a post-racial era in Amerikkka. I can only speak for the Black experience and what I will say is the post-racial era is a myth. Slavery is very present and continues to terrorize us in legally defensible, obvious, and incredibly insidious ways. This experience was 17 years ago for me, and the world only got the memo that there is a significant problem in 2020. What does this say about our humanity? What does this say about the systems and structures guiding the world of work? I will let you meditate on that.

> ***Purposeful Human Reflection:*** *It's time for Corporate Amerikkka to wake up! Admit that your systems and structures were designed to keep certain groups marginalized so that White, Christian, Heterosexual Men, can thrive first, and then their counterparts: White, Heterosexual, Christian women. Everyone else gets in where they fit in. That is the pecking order. No one can debate me on this. It is infuriating to be subject to an ecosystem that you have no choice but to be a part of*

because if not, how else can you survive? When everything in that ecosystem is designed to destroy you from the inside out while you collect just enough money to be in debt. Indebted to the job, indebted to an economy that feasts on you, indebted to people bred to destroy you at all costs. What becomes of the psyche of the Black person and really any of the other communities of color being predisposed to this narrative over the course of a career? You're seeing it now. It looks like rebel elegance and revolution. If you look like me and any of this resonates: Resist, Rebel, and Stay Resilient. We are the change we have been waiting for.

This last reflection was a doozy. If you identify as Black, Indigenous, Latino, Latinx, Latine, AAPI, and any community of color I missed, what are some experiences you have had like this? Have you made peace with it? How did it change the way you saw work and your place in society?

White folx- This is your moment to reflect on what you just read. What needs to be changed? How will you commit to being a trusted ally and steward of better practices, and, more importantly, societal change?

Use the space below to document your purposeful human reflections.

"GETTING INTO THE CAREER GROOVE"

Beyond the circus days of Aerotek, I returned to my roots, returning to healthcare. After that tumultuous yet somewhat rewarding experience, my days in Staffing with all of its greed and need for extraordinary sales prowess were over. It only seemed fitting that I would return to the lakes and rivers that I was used to. I took a stab at working for Bayada Nurses. It was homecare, so it was providing me another slice of healthcare I had yet to touch. This time, I made sure the job was on Long Island so I could drive, and my focus was Personnel/HR related, not selling or immature foolishness. My role was as a Personnel Coordinator/Recruiter. The thing I loved most about the position is I had a lot of autonomy to structure my work and days as I saw fit. They had a formal orientation process that required me to go to King of Prussia, Pennsylvania, for a weeklong training at their Corporate Offices. It was refreshing. The formality that I was onboarded with was more aligned with what I wanted and dare I say expected when I started at Aerotek, but I digress.

This was the first time I had driven myself a distance for work, so that in and of itself was exciting. Having the ability to meet my counterparts in other regions and hear about the valuable work our nurses were doing on the frontline was likely the first time I understood the concept of culture and the value of ensuring that the company's mission and vision are articulated well right from the start.

I remember returning with a few more friends to my credit and feeling committed to doing my best by the company. Our Director of Nursing was hired when I was. I was indoctrinated like most people at that time into thinking that your title and position in a company dictate the quality of your acumen and your ability to lead. I was terribly mistaken. What I quickly learned upon returning from orientation was that our office was the awkward and much less profitable stepchild of the organization. Our leaders were not respected and this Director of Nursing, while extremely sweet and nice, was ill-equipped to lead us out of a situation already exacerbated by politics and poor management. Unfortunately, what I observed in this job is that niceness must be well-placed and not served up copiously in hopes that it will garner you respect.

We had nurses that were committing fraud, PCA's who were deviating from the care plans and doing whatever they pleased. We had patients who were bed ridden explicitly requesting white nurses even though we had none who were willing to travel to them. I mean, how are you going to be bed ridden with diabetic wounds and have the audacity to say you don't want an available Black nurse? This was condoned pretty much up until I arrived. With all of this calamity, I soon realized that we needed a formal orientation process for the office to ensure that our employees understood the mission and vision of the organization, but also got the necessary training upfront to encourage better patient outcomes. I didn't have any experience prior to this moment in time developing orientations, just my undergrad experience. I developed our new orientation and onboarding process. I requested a budget to fund a few perks for our new employees; I included in-service education to ensure they earned credits for approved learning from the beginning, and I coached each of our staff members on the importance of being a part of the process.

Our orientations were a success and allowed for much greater insight and controls around employee performance. I even started going out with the nurses to do skills evaluations. This was the first time I understood that you can lead from wherever you sit. Hierarchy and titles don't mean a thing when the blind is leading the blind. I understood People Operations, and I owned the hell out of that. Eventually, I would go on to become a translator for their in-services that were transcribed into Spanish for our Spanish-Speaking Employees. That was a gig I did for an entire year even after I left the organization. Bayada taught me to bet on myself and to not be afraid to expand in different directions even if I didn't have full command of the function yet.

> ***Purposeful Human Reflection:*** *If you're waiting on the perfect experience at work, you will be waiting a long time. There is something to going through a few cycles of chaos in your career. It provides you with an opportunity to sink or swim. Preparation has its place, but I can honestly say I learned more about myself and others in imperfect circumstances. Trust what you know. Trust your abilities and never be afraid to innovate on the fly. Game changers provide solutions and roll up their sleeves so their team can survive another day. Is it easy? No. Is it rewarding? Hell yeah!*
>
> *Don't stop, get it... get it... let us reflect together, purposeful humans. Do you enjoy solving problems? What do you think prevents you from stepping into your power in moments of chaos, whether perceived or actual? How would it feel to have your ideas heard and what could it do for your confidence?*

Use the space below to document your purposeful human reflections.

"DON'T STOP BELIEVIN'"

September 27, 2015

I am clear that I have to let go of any negative energy or thoughts and always try to see the brighter side of things. Life is precious and beautiful. When you stop believing in your ability to become better, you have lost the race. Every day I wake up, I have another opportunity to get it right.

"HELL HATH NO FURY LIKE AN INTIMIDATED WOMAN"

Hindsight is truly 20/20. It took me quite a few years to come to the realization that I was encountering the same archetype of a boss in different ways in each of my last three jobs. The archetype is the following: All were women, white women who used their charm and wit to rise the ranks. Even though they all rose to various semblances of success in their respective careers, there was a deep-seated insecurity that caused them to create superficial connections with their employees and even more so with their employees who are women. If I'm honest, none of these women were particularly astute in their areas of expertise, nor were they effective as leaders. They did just enough, smiled just enough, and gently stroked the egos of the right people (mostly white men) to secure their places in the organizations they served.

In each of those jobs, I rose to prominence quickly and diligently. I was getting progressively better at my craft. I was becoming more curious about the problems I was capable of solving and excited for the myriad of innovative ways I could expand my contributions. To most leaders, my approach and mindset regarding my body of work would be an asset. In hindsight, I was an asset. However, when your good work moves beyond being just good enough to make your boss look good, but instead visible to leaders above their pay grade; now you become a threat that must be eliminated and so it goes.

Let me give you a sense of some of the things I endured at the hands of these wounded characters in my life. I worked for North Shore LIJ, now Northwell Health, in 2008. I took a step down from being a full-fledged recruiter to being a TA coordinator because I was six months pregnant with my first child and I wanted the benefit of less stress and less responsibility whilst incubating my little Libra princess-to-be. When someone takes a step back in their career for personal reasons, it is in no way a reflection of any diminished intelligence, capability, or acumen. It was a professional reprieve. It didn't take too much longer after returning to work from maternity leave that I was promoted to Recruiter. Looking back, I feel the decision to promote me was both based on my ability and the quality of my work, but also because their turnover for recruiters was so high that they were trying to stop the hemorrhaging by putting a competent person in the role.

I expressed my concerns about the things I saw other Recruiters going through and took great care to communicate my need for that experience to be different. For a time, it was great. I got along just fine with the Director of Talent Acquisition, or so I thought. In fairness, I was warned by a few of my peers to be careful with her and that she can turn on you for virtually nothing. I kept that intel in my back pocket as I navigated her. One day, there was an email sent from one of the departments about my handling of a job. It wasn't irregular for hiring managers to express their displeasure with our work. We were a centralized HR function for over forty facilities handling every vacant position across a variety of functions, both union and non-union. Every recruiter carried over eighty-plus requisitions hiring the masses weekly, often blind to the realities at the sites, grossly under-resourced, and very much against the best interest of the organization with the constant coercion of focusing on "VIP hires." The displeasure with TA was known, communicated, and felt. Nevertheless, the narrative that was handed to my Director of TA was missing many pieces. I was brought into her office and berated not only about what was shared with her, but she attacked me personally, sharing that she felt my "personal life and professional pursuits were impeding my ability to be effective." Here's what precipitated that: I started to back off of too much personal conversation with her. I took my peers' advice and treaded lightly. That retreat was noticed and not appreciated. Additionally, I had been granted clearance upon returning from my maternity leave to take up an HR/Recruitment-focused certification through Cornell ILR. I not only garnered one recruitment certificate, I ended up with five eventually, but my constant requests to take new courses at their Center of Learning, plus my work ethic spelled trouble for her in her own mind. The way she ripped into me behind closed doors actually brought me to tears; a first for me in a professional setting. If you know anything about me, once you cause me to cry, the next emotion for me is anger for causing that emotion in me. For me, it's like you forced your way to get a glimpse of my vulnerability and now I must discard you. I kid, but that can be how it feels. The extremes in her demeanor from berating me to consoling me upon the sight of my tears were far more dastardly than I knew in that moment. She had found a way to break my spirit, and she would use different tactics for the next nine months or so to continue on that path.

The next time she struck was when I was brought in for my performance evaluation, and I went in thinking I will hear all the great things, all to be told I was being mean to my TA coordinator and made her cry. It never happened! When I asked her to provide a date, the date in question was a day I wasn't even at work, I was home sick. How can I be terrorizing my coordinator while at home and nursing myself back to health? I told her I wasn't accepting the evaluation or signing it. When I went to my coordinator and asked her about this incident, she said she had no clue what she was speaking about. It was then that I understood I was being set up.

When I went back to her with the conversation I had with my coordinator, she refused to change her evaluation. I told her I would go up the ranks if needed, and I did.

When I did, the business partner, Dahlys Oetting, heard my story and proceeded to ask me if I wanted to "keep this in the family" before escalating it further. I told her I was sure I wanted to escalate the issue. She in turn said, "this will not bode well for your career here." Imagine being told this by someone who is charged with ensuring employees are being treated fairly and not in just any old department but HR. This is also someone who was a contributor to the smoke and mirrors of this organization whose tagline at the time was "hope lives here." Virtually no one who worked in Central HR between 2006 and 2010 would agree. I watched colleagues taken out on stretchers due to the stress of the job. I opened my office to peers to be able to close the door, vent, and sometimes cry.

Mrs. Oetting was a thug, but she spoke the truth. The escalation never benefited me. Actually, it caused a shit storm and a license for three White Women and one Asian woman to bully me until I eventually couldn't take it any longer and left the organization. The Director of TA drowned me in work only to ask why things weren't filled in a certain timeframe, berated me behind closed doors, set up meetings I was supposed to attend only to cancel them and spin me around.

Back then the Bible and I were close compadres. You know something is wrong when I would have to steal away to the bathroom to read a Psalm to get through the day. I was prepared to prop and fold at Target, abandoning HR altogether to preserve my sanity. Luckily and quite cosmically, I landed a job at Brookhaven National Laboratory (BNL) after using one of our recruiting firms to place me there in 2010.

At BNL, I found some peace but didn't quite escape the bruised egos of White Women and surprisingly Black Women who play respectability politics to gain ground in the fight for equity in the workforce. Let me frankly say that it is a hell of a mind-fuck to have to take orders and direction from women who you are more educated than and who were only as relevant as their tenure dictates. BNL is where I soared. It was a slower environment and so my corporate chops put me ahead of the curve in a workforce that was very much complacent and entitled. What my then boss felt was "niche" and "hard-to-fill" was not as much of a challenge for me. Even difficult hiring managers were less challenging; I had been there, done that and had a confidence grounded in my training and professional experience. I had also come online and started to build a personal brand for myself based on my professional interests and background. Exposing myself to a global audience and having the ability to share with others in my field outside of the confines of the organizations I served was a wildly new circumstance and one that excited me.

My acumen across pretty much every function in HR plus my operational and strategic mindset made me a gold mine for my boss. She wasn't looking to destroy me, but she damn well buffered her deficits by poaching and peddling my work as if it was her own. She had her favorites on the team. If money were a sign of her adoration for me, I was likely her least favorite, and yet I was performing two other roles than what I was hired to do. I was at BNL for four years. During one performance evaluation period, I asked for a change to my job description, because I was doing HRIS analyst work. She had the audacity to speak to me about the Compensation Manager being the key partner for that role. I articulated every project, the time I spent managing our systems, and trainings I designed. Nice man, but he had not contributed one iota to any of those efforts. A warning came after my frankness: "be careful." The truth was the truth, and I wanted my due for my effort. She finally gave in and allowed me to change my title.

Not to speak about race, but let's talk about race. This was a white woman with a high school diploma with Director of HR decision-making power and earning director salary with very little clue of how HR as a discipline was evolving and not much of an operational business sense. The Compensation Manager she spoke of was a white man. Far more astute in his respective function and earning top dollars and accolades too. All the same, he had not been equipped or motivated to bring the lab into the 21st century of technology in the way I did. Let this be a clear example of what I mentioned earlier about the socio-economic pecking order and how White people take care of White people for the most part. There are very few who see fit to extend the courtesies they extend one another, and it only happens this way if they were raised by people who were vehemently against oppressing people of color, or they grew up in racist households and have chosen a different path out of utter annoyance for what their bloodlines represent.

When I eventually put in my resignation at BNL in 2014, I had done a lot of good things at the lab. Their diversity outreach efforts and hiring had much improved based on partnerships I walked in the door with and others I had cultivated while there. They were bringing on their first SaaS ATS due to my urging and efforts. Relationships with some of our more prominent scientists/hiring managers were better because I created a different sort of partnership and understanding with them. Their African American Affinity Group (AAAG) was well on its way to being a solid resource group for both Black people hired at the lab and those to come in the future.

Outside of BNL, my professional portfolio was shaping up nicely. Talent Think Innovations, my consulting firm, was about a year into its existence and thriving. From a PR perspective, I had garnered my first major magazine while on maternity leave. That was the year I landed myself in Black

Enterprise. Obviously, when I returned to work, I shared my good news with peers and AAAG. I even had a clipping of the spread hung up in my cube. I came in a weekend not long from putting in my resignation and noticed someone had written on it. The excuse I was given was that one of my peers' children mistakenly did it. In the weeks to come as I finished up my time with them, I had to hear about how this same boss of mine was saying I built my brand on company time. If she only knew how many days I was up at 6am to do radio spots in the UK, the nights I worked through dinner and well after putting my young children to sleep, the lunch times I used to record podcasts or PTO I took to conduct a webinar, she would have shut her mouth.

BNL was and is a set-it-and-forget-it place to work. Most of the people at her level went to work there in their late teens and never left. It isn't a place that ruffles your feathers much; people take their lunches promptly at 12 or 1pm and leave promptly at 5pm. The work you do there has exponential implications for the U.S. and the world at large. I can say I supported cutting-edge research, but as an organization, BNL is where a young person's dreams and professional pursuits went to die a slow death. I am fortunate that I had guides and mentors to help me see that this was true for me.

A word on the Black Women Leaders I encountered at BNL. It was at Northwell that I got a glimpse of the wayward ways Black leadership is cultivated in large organizations, but it would be at BNL where it became crystal clear to me what systems, structures, and shenanigans fuel Black Leadership at the enterprise-level. On one hand, you come across some leaders who eloquently embody the balance between preserving who they are despite the inertia pulling them to conform to white standards. These leaders typically go on to shift the dynamics of what it means to work while being Black. Conversely, you have these legacy-types within organizations who are quietly passionate about what is wrong but play the white game successfully and equally expect younger Black professionals to sell their souls in kind for a title, money, marginal respect, and perceived influence. I met both types at both Northwell and BNL and quite frankly they irked me more than the white folks who were doing their usual waltz of white privilege. I have come to expect a certain amount of Loki-like (Nordic God of Trickery) behavior from white people in general, it's known and predictable. However, it is extremely gross when the gatekeepers of diversity, equity, inclusion, and belonging look like you and have traded in the good fight for becoming a workforce massa of sorts who has no real power other than passing on perverse mindsets and behaviors of conformity.

In short, we melanated people have to examine our thirst for being recognized in white spaces and how it often serves as an impediment to the personal and professional progress of future generations of BIPOC professionals whereby relevance in your career can be obtained without it detracting from one's identity and self-worth.

Do I believe that the feminine energies I detailed here were intimidated by me? Yes. Somewhere in their psyche, they convinced themselves that my knowledge, skills, and abilities were an affront to their success and reputation. The humor in it all is that my end game was bigger than their thankless leadership roles. When there is a perceived threat, it must be eliminated, and that is precisely what they did, whether by creating conditions that were unbearable for me to work in or by creating narratives about who I was and my contributions to put a stain on my name.

The elegance of all these stories is that my life got better after each of these experiences. My professional portfolio and career soared because I never let these moments in time deter me from what I knew I was capable of. I won't waste space detailing what became of them here. Let's just say things didn't exactly work out the way they envisioned it. The universe is pettier than I will ever be.

Evolving Soul Reflection: *Power given to the wrong people will always create toxic conditions. Marginalization and oppression are conceptually bad parenting relationships. In this way, there will always be a percentage of people who have been oppressed or marginalized that will become the "parent," the oppressor. They will both consciously and unconsciously do to others what was done to them. In the case of my story, women would be the group in question. We have been marginalized for decades and yet if you speak to people on the ground about what happens when some of them get the power and prestige, it goes the way of what I just detailed. What I have the benefit of knowing today is these women were wounded and insecure in many ways, which caused them to react to me in the manner that they did. More importantly, they had a divine assignment and they executed. I would have stayed at any of those jobs and did the normal thing of trying to prove my worth to rise the ranks. Had the conditions I endured not been created by them, I may never have started my own company and taken a chance on myself. They did what they were designed to do. Everything is always working for us, never against us.*

I call this portion of the book "Corporate Amerikkka: The House of Cards" playing a bit on the show "House of Cards." If you ever watched, you know that the whole show is a compelling yet frightening window into the politics within the politics and what power drives some people to do to retain it. My story is your story. I have traveled and spoken to enough people through the years to know my experiences in Corporate Amerikkka aren't figments of my imagination. There are women and men alike experiencing characters like this every day. The bigger question for you as you are reading this is: What are these experiences and characters meant to teach you? Is it time to move on totally or perhaps into a different department? If yes, start to plan your best next move. What specific steps can you take today to get you where you need to be?

Use the space below to document your purposeful human reflections.

“CLEARING THE AIR”

February 23, 2015

I am excited for the possibility my company has. Every day, I do my best to position myself such that my knowledge and abilities will be recognized. Professionally, I am well on my way and love the variety of work I do. I feel great and on top of the world some days, and other days I feel like my world is crashing down on me. I genuinely feel that I have worked hard and tirelessly to be where I am today. I understand that adversity is necessary to realize success, but it feels like I have been in limbo for a long time. Setbacks make me feel like I’m a failure; like I have made the wrong decisions. It’s a place of hurt and sorrow and hopelessness that I would not wish on my worst enemy. What I want is simple. I want to have the money to live and enjoy life on my own terms. I feel like money controls me and my life. It isn’t a good feeling. I feel at times I am being punished somehow and I don’t have a clue why. I am richer than most in that I am healthy and have healthy kids and a spouse that loves me unconditionally. You can’t put a price on that. However, we want to travel, pay our debts, give back to the less fortunate, eat in nice places, and just enjoy our lives. We’re happy, we’ve worked hard, and now we want to enjoy some things in return for our trials and adversity. I can appreciate rain, snow, but it would be nice to have more sunny days, more joy. I want to never have a debt again and never owe a soul. I want to walk into a store and choose what I need, never worrying about whether I can afford it. I want to work with great people, doing work that improves the world at large. I want my children to have what they need and some of what they want, too. I want to experience this beautiful life with my husband exploring new places, things, people, and food.

Life has felt heavy and difficult. I want to feel light and free. I deserve to have my business succeed. I deserve to have time to care for my kids the way I see fit. I deserve a life without constraints or boundaries.

The signs that something great is coming are there. I'm trying to keep moving and striving. Having faith is hard, but it works, and I am trying to have more of it. Today I cried a lot, and it was needed. I needed to feel what I have been avoiding. Today, I choose to be vulnerable and human. I'm not perfect and I am doing the best that I can. I am very hard on myself, and I need to practice what I preach. That starts with loving myself fully and unconditionally.

I am human. I make mistakes and it's alright. Everything is alright.

Reading this reflection back stirs up so many emotions within me. On one hand, I'm catapulted back there immediately remembering this year, and all I endured. In another regard, I know much more about why I had some of those struggles back then, and that infuriates me.

I started my business Talent Think Innovations in 2013. I was still working for Brookhaven National Laboratory (BNL) at the time. Truthfully, this business was on a twenty-year plan. I always said I would rise the ranks to at least a CHRO, and by the time my husband retired, I would be ready to consult for myself. The absurdity of that line of thinking is that I thought my plan was better than the divine master plan. The reality of things is my plan was safe, extremely linear, and left no room for the serendipity that life throws our way.

Being a CHRO was a dream I gave up long before I was halfway through my four-year stint at BNL. It just seemed like more headaches than it was worth and didn't provide me with the depth and breadth of work I would have been happy with. My mindset about money and prestige had changed. I wasn't as easily wooed by a fancy title. The plan I had was further diminished by the fact that I would never reach the point of seeing my then husband's retirement because I would end up divorcing him by 2019. Remember the dream was coming to fruition by 2025. The plan had already drastically changed eight years prior to that. Whoops!

All the things I thought I needed to be properly prepared to run a successful business never happened. What did happen was a lack of upward mobility and stagnancy at BNL, Hurricane Sandy in 2012, and the government shutdown of 2013 that nearly furloughed me and my peers. It was those three occurrences and a lot of great advice and incessant nudging from friends and mentors that I decided to take the leap into working for myself.

I tested the viability of Talent Think Innovations throughout 2013 and 2014. I even took clients on my maternity leave when I felt better and up to it. By the time I returned to work from maternity leave in September 2014, BNL was screwing with my work from home days and one of my major projects was in shambles. I reached out to my husband at the time and expressed my gripes about my return to work and my desire to go full time in the business. He said, "think about it overnight. If you still feel like resigning in the morning, put in your resignation." My resignation was typed and signed by that evening. I resigned from BNL that October and was fortunate to start working with IBM the next week.

At that time, I was still on Facebook. I remember being in an HR-related group that chronicled all upcoming HR events.

I saw this event called IBM New Way to Work that was happening in NY. I followed the breadcrumbs and realized it was being run by Bryan Kramer of Purematter. We were connected on Twitter and had chatted there sparingly, so I went to Twitter and reached out to him on DM to inquire about it. He explained they were pulling together experts to work with IBM to reimagine the future of work. Unfortunately, he had also shared that their participant slots were full, but told me he would keep me in mind. I thanked him and went to sleep.

The next morning, I woke up to a DM from him saying, "You're in," send me your email and info.

BNL had zero respect for the four-week notice I provided and there was no value in me remaining there an additional week. I revised my resignation and cut my resignation back by a week so I could go work with IBM. I left BNL on a Friday and that following Monday, a car came to pick me up to attend my first session and dinner with IBM.

I had a few clients that I had in rotation at that time, but their work eventually concluded. By the time 2015 rolled around, I had no client work, this brand-new business, and the bills and pressure were mounting. I started to be paralyzed by fear. I questioned if I had made the right decision to leave my steady paycheck at BNL. As a result, I started entertaining opportunities again. I had a screening call for a Senior Recruiter position and just listening to the duties and time of report was enough to depress me. I remember getting off of the screening and just falling to my knees in tears. I told myself that I had to make a decision. It was either stay the course or take one of these soul-sucking jobs. I decided to stay the course. Within a few weeks, opportunities and client work started coming my way out of nowhere.

The first two years in business were tough, not necessarily because of a lack of preparation, but because I needed to cultivate an unwavering belief in myself and what I was building. It was also difficult because I was with someone who was supportive but also sabotaging us financially and otherwise making it difficult to stay afloat. Our debts and lack of available money was crippling. There is nothing more disorienting than to be coming into your season and being at the top of your game as a public figure, but to have to go home to a financial reality that told a much different story.

You don't truly develop an appreciation for faith until it is all you have left. When shame is palpable and isolation feels the safest, faith is the only thing standing in the gap for you and with you as you straddle sanity and complete despair. It is at this point that you have met your ground zero, that place where so much is falling apart so rapidly that all you have left is your optimism and the belief that better is possible.

I always call 2015 my "Year of Tears" because never in my life had I cried as much as I did that year. I cried happy tears for the major strides I made in business that year and I cried in despair for the way my home life never seemed to reflect the person I was becoming. My husband would always say, "don't cry, everything will be alright...we will figure things out." What I didn't know then was it would never get better if I was unprepared to see that he was at the root of our problems. He also knew it would never get better because he was the only one that knew the myriad of ways he was funneling money out of our household to support his toxic habits and an outside child, as I would much later find out.

2015 was also the year I would experience burnout for the first time ever. The exhilaration of career progress coupled with the trauma of financial woes is a winning recipe for your body to give out on you. I remember waking up one day in October 2015 with rapid heart palpitations that felt like what I imagine a heart attack feels like and an extreme fatigue I couldn't quite shake. I thought many times I should go to the ER, but the prideful side of me said take your time with it, Google the symptoms, and remember you have these three children to look after.

I learned that those palpitations were panic attacks, and I had a harsh awakening that year that nothing I was doing was sustainable. This was the true precipice of my spiritual awakening and all the transformation that followed from it.

Evolving Soul Reflection: *We all have seasons where we aren't operating in the ideal circumstances, and we aren't exactly our best selves. When I started Talent Think Innovations, I was given the money to get my LLC by my mom and my aunt. My uncle was kind enough to build out my first website and logo so I would have some digital property ahead of attending my first major conference. I had very little to get started, but also what I had was all I required to create a foundation for success. The dark moments show up to allow you to incubate, reflect, and make the necessary changes and pivots so you grow into your light accordingly.*

What have been some of your darkest moments? What place did faith have in your process? How have those dark moments changed you for the better?

Use the space below to document your evolving soul reflections. Hugging you from a distance.

BECOMING "ME"

April 9th, 2018

I've spent this past weekend feeling both mentally and physically withdrawn. The extent of my tiredness is extreme and the depth of my thoughts limitless. Love these days is both confusing and jarring. It has cracked the veneer I have gotten crafty at creating between myself and vulnerability. Now, there is both sunshine and darkness that seep through the cracks. Depending on which it is, I either want to run through the meadows with glee or lay myself on the ground and weep sorrowfully. I am feeling all my feelings as if I have spent the last 34 years of my life numb and never feeling at all. I am suddenly having to face parts of myself I never knew existed. How exciting, yet terrifying it is to wake up to new versions of yourself every day having to decide what you want to keep and which parts of yourself you want to throw away. I am changing, evolving, and transforming daily. All I can do now is show up, face it, and embrace it. It is all very tortuous and at the same time it is love that has done all of this. I have no idea what I am supposed to do with these new feelings and revelations about myself.

Do I sit with them? Some part of me says "yes." Today, that is all I can do. So, I will sit and bask in the glory of my becoming, but I will also weep maybe because I know that an older, more comfortable version of me is gone. I need to mourn her and weep some more so I can arrive to celebrate a newer, better version of me someday soon.

"TOO MANY F**KING THOUGHTS"

February 28th, 2019

Thinking is overdone and overused in our society. We have traded true connection to ourselves, emotions, feelings, and others for logic and intellectual discourse.

Don't get me wrong, I am a cerebral being through and through. The issue comes in when we are unaware that our thinking creates what we see. Our lack of awareness about that phenomenon means we are often creating more of what we don't want than what we want (thank you Abraham-Hicks for re-parenting me). It is the reason that life coaches, IG psychologists, therapists, and self-help book authors who are disseminating copious numbers of banal quotes are all the rage at the moment.

When you finally find that having more thoughts is actually failing you, you become more intentional and observant of what you think. In my case, having all of the thoughts was reinforced as a positive characteristic in my family and throughout my education. Our society places a high value on people who are thinkers and have a seemingly endless stream of thoughts to pepper us with. Knowing that your thoughts become things puts you in a powerful position on this planet. Arguably, that knowing will be one of the most impactful prongs to our success as a species in the next decade. This means you now have no other choice but to select fewer thoughts and you have a duty to ensure that they are your best.

My work is mentally intensive. I'm an analyst, strategist, visionary, and medicine woman, so full use of my neurons and synapses is necessary most days. I am working hard this year to allow my mind to rest more.

We need to trust that not everything requires our meddling, whether mental or otherwise. There is a delicate balance of doing and being that we have yet to achieve as humans. As we all learned about "homeostasis" in grade school, we ought to remember it as our collective call to strike a balance in all aspects of life.

As such, it's a grand time to take a slight step back and let the universe work on our behalf. If you are an empath, healer, lightworker, Black, or Indigenous you have been putting in work for forever. Rest and rest some more. Even if you are none of those things and your mind is tired, weary, and cluttered. Rest. There is progress and productivity in resting and being still.

> ***Find some place peaceful so we can reflect together, purposeful humans.*** *How are you prioritizing rest currently? Do you get enough sleep at night? If not, how can you do better with this? How can you shift your mindset on rest in your life?*

Use the space below to document your purposeful human reflections.

I NEED YOU
TO KNOW
YOU ARE
SO LOVED
AND
PROTECTED.

“THE ANCESTRAL EYE”

My mom said that when I was born something shifted with the grandparents. A different kind of bond was formed. Thinking about my relationships with them I can say that is absolutely true. On both sides of my family, I am the oldest of the grandchildren. I knew early on there was something special between us because of what they trusted me with. I was probably the only grandchild who grew up the most West-Indian. It was made clear that academics were paramount to my success in this country and next to that was my ability to care for myself.

There was no sleeping in late on their watch. In hindsight, much of the time I had the privilege of spending with them was a crash course on life. From learning from my Grandpa Wills about the way our food was being compromised long before the vegan and plant-based movements became a thing to my Grandma Wills teaching me how to garden and about different herbs and their abilities to heal us, I was being trained up as a new ancestor.

We had an understanding. My mind and reasoning were well ahead of my time. Speaking to any of my grandparents gave me the spirit to keep going. They affirmed me and gave me the necessary lifelines to continue spreading my light. I remember being in elementary school and being made fun of for enjoying library time. If you were a good student, one of the rewards was getting to spend time at the library solo. I didn't know a damn thing about being an introvert, but for my quiet, brainy soul this was clutch. I took advantage of it often. I told my Grandma Wills that I felt unlike the other kids. My joy was in learning and reading. It opened up new worlds of knowledge for me. She told me, "You don't worry about those kids. Stay focused on your studies and it is going to carry you far." She said, "I am praying every day for you and your brother's safe keeping. The Lord will carry you." At times, I think they would have preferred I didn't have to take on this role of the new ancestor, but they too had an assignment to prepare me not only for my destined path, but for the role I would have to assume in our family and eventually as the matriarch of my own.

How do I know I am the new ancestor?

I am the keeper of my family's traditions, culture, and secrets on both sides. This will likely rub some the wrong way, but I know what frustrated my grandparents about certain members in the family. I know their hurts and the heartbreak each of them took to their respective graves. They started off as my confidantes, but later in each of their lives I became that confidante to them too. We spoke often and like old friends that had lived many lifetimes together. They kept after me because they knew I was not only the one to keep their influence alive, but they also trusted me to shift any dynamics that were soiling our bloodline. They trusted me to do what they couldn't.

I lost both my Papi and Grandpa Wills within a year and a half of one another. Each took a piece of my soul when they left. It was maybe three to four years after each of their transitions that they came to me in a dream, smiling and telling me how proud they were of me. It was pre-awakening, so that was the safest way for them to tell me they were alright and that they had my back. About two years ago, I started seeing "527" a ton. It didn't dawn on me why until my Ancestry DNA started sending me nearly daily hints of a relative. Every time I clicked on the email it was my Grandpa Wills' name. At this time, I started going to Reiki as well, and my girlfriend, Cashel, had mentioned that my grandparents were around me and wanting to help. I bawled like a baby. My Grandpa is still around. He never left me to do life without him. He was letting me know he has his ancestral eye on me and mine.

It was around this time that I started my altar. Instead of hiding the faces of those who sustained me on Earth for a finite time, I learned to acknowledge and celebrate them daily. I also learned that a transition beyond the physical is just that, a transition. The first law of thermodynamics states that "energy can be changed from one form to another, but it cannot be created or destroyed." The quantity of energy in the universe remains constant always and in all ways. So, while the physical loss feels like a knife in our hearts, there is solace in knowing that the love and connection can never be extinguished.

I listen for a whisper in the wind, a soul urge to be in nature, a song they send me on shuffle, and most importantly, I feel my way through the ethers for a mostly invisible but palpable connection to my loved ones who may be gone but have never forgotten me as they rest eternally.

MOTHERHOOD BY DEFAULT

When I left Malverne High School, I had high hopes of becoming a world-renowned biochemist that would go on to live abroad happily and maybe snag an artsy, yet modern man while I was at it. Instead, I was met with my parent's crumbling marriage on the heels of my liberation into young adulthood, which precipitated some decisions that would affect me both positively and negatively for a long time to come. In hindsight, I suppose I could have or should have been selfish and did what I wanted anyway. To be fair, I had also fallen in love with my children's dad/future husband whom we will refer to as "Venom Pain." The combination of young love and my perceived sense of duty made me choose Hofstra University because it was local and meant I could see where this young love would lead me while also allowing me to stick around for my brother (who at the time) was extremely vulnerable and turbulent. I spent my 4 years at Hofstra excelling in every way imaginable but also learning what I truly desired to learn. I journeyed through one change to my major, supporting my family through a difficult divorce proceeding, culminating with the sudden death of my grandfather who I called "Papi."

When your mother decides to move out of the house and you are 18 with a father on the heels of retirement and a 13-year-old sibling who can't understand what's happening, you step up to fill in all the holes in the sinking ship, or at least that is what I did. I became the pseudo-wife, cooking, food shopping, and shouldering my father's emotional pain as he went through his divorce. At the same time, my brother became a rebel of epic proportions that I now had significant responsibility for. I never asked for the responsibility, and yet I shudder to think what would have become of him without me being there. The divorce was tough. My relationship with my mother was strained as I struggled to understand her decisions and approach. As if it wasn't enough torment to deal with moving her out and our estranged relationship, I became the sounding board for every family member who held an opinion of my parents' then 17-year marriage. No matter what transpires in the dissolution of a family unit, no child wants to hear how their parents should have never had kids. Sure, my parents were oil and water. I learned much later that trauma and patriarchal expectation in partnerships are anything but easy. Can we not just chalk an ending of a union up to growing apart or some other relational factor without resorting to wishing away mine and my brother's lives?

The day my parents' divorce was final, I came along with my dad and sat in the car. It is a rather strange event when your mother and her lawyer (who was also a family friend) walk up matter-of-factly to say "good morning" before entering the courthouse to dissolve the family unit. Without getting too deep, words were exchanged, and I was numb and full of rage. Back then, my unmanaged rage could lead to an asthmatic episode. Imagine my parents' horror and appreciate the irony that the very same day the divorce became final, they both were met with me having an asthma attack that landed me in the ER at Winthrop Hospital. Both were present, and it was the first time I realized civility is necessary when dissolving a relationship where kids are involved. The marriage certificate may become a relic, but your bond is forever, whether you like your co-parent or not. As a co-parent myself, I can appreciate this experience for illustrating exactly what I didn't want to emulate. When you know better, you have a duty to do better.

My additional clarity on that life event today is that the attack was my younger body's response to mothering a teenage sibling, my father, and in some regards my mother. It gets clearer later in my story how this foundation both helped and hurt.

You may feel sorry for me after reading this. The wounded inner child in me selfishly wants the pity party, but the more evolved me says impart a lesson. The thing I learned in having my own children is that it requires intention. Daily, I strive to use my traumas as a reminder of the ways in which I must be intentional about not repeating cycles and passing on generational pain. I am far from perfect, and my parents were far from being horrible. Hurt people hurt people, and it takes a great deal of courage to deviate from the standard you've always known. I believe, for the most part, my parents did the best with what they knew. Additionally, I think there was an emotional laziness they found comfort in because I was so astute in illuminating and addressing the black holes in our family dynamics. That aside, it was never my responsibility to unpack their traumas, fill in their deficits, or even be the voice of reason. Generational trauma is real and underdeveloped psyches are never a recipe for great parenting. It's important that I call a spade a spade so any of you reading don't get into the nasty habit of normalizing harm. What I know today is whatever I suffered was to illuminate the generational traumas needing to be cleared. It was also a foreshadowing of the ways cycles and lessons have an insidious way of showing up again to ensure we learn what's best for us once and for all.

Evolving Soul Reflection: *Sometimes we are casualties of a series of poor decisions made by our parents and/or loved ones. The intent often isn't personal, but our emotions, mind, and sensibilities know nothing different. What often feels like an unfortunate set of circumstances is likely preparation for your blessings to come. Steer your ship forward as best as you can and soon you will look back at your perceived misgivings as constellations leading you to where you were meant to be.*

What's your parents' story? Whether positive, negative, or mixed, spend some time reflecting upon your own journey with your parents and what they have taught you to date. Reflect some more on the discussion of templates for life and see what comes up for you.

Use the space below to document your evolving soul reflections.

"GIVING BIRTH TO MYSELF"

I'm a mom of three children. I started my motherhood journey at 24 with intention and excitement for the little beings that "Venom Pain" and I would produce. I had already graduated and was well on my way in my career working for NES Healthcare. Everyone told me about the sleepless nights, contractions, and the responsibility of having to look after a whole other human being. What no one shared was the transformation you undergo throughout the process both psychologically and emotionally.

Here's how life is full of tricks. I ended up having three c-sections because the U.S. sees healthcare as a payday rather than a modality of preserving its citizens. Let's settle in with the fact that the c-sections gave me no frame of reference for what a contraction felt like, so by the time I had my youngest daughter in 2012, I was working and going about my days never realizing that those sharp pains I was having were contractions. She came ten days early via an emergency c-section and my oldest daughter came ten days late. My son came right on time like the little prince he is. Each of these humans expanded my ability to love in ways I never thought imaginable. I had to redefine what perfection and success looked like for myself. They didn't curtail my dreams, but rather they were constant reminders that anything was possible in my life. I started to think heavily on the kind of woman I wanted to exemplify for each of them and the things I never wanted to repeat as a mother based on my own upbringing. The paradox of motherhood is there is no playbook on how to do it. You either find yourself looking backwards, doing your best to be everything that you have experienced through your own parents, or you aim to distance yourself from those attributes which requires an entirely new ethos for parenting for which you have no blueprint. It's a lot of work and it can be scary.

What I ended up realizing is that raising kids of the latter 2000s and 2010s is a whole other ballgame. It requires empathy, creativity, and an agile mind to keep up with the twists and turns of our world. I came into recognition that I didn't have to try so hard to be the opposite of my own mother, but rather my focus needed to be squarely on the parenting my kids wanted and needed. I became the mother I needed, and it has worked out. Each of those kids are a mish-mosh of me and their dad in ways we have expressed ourselves and ways we have yet to express ourselves. Time is never on your side when you are feeding and caring for humans and so I have chosen to consciously parent them, taking the best of what my mom, grandmothers, and other women gave me while putting my own remix on it.

They see me and I see them. My children are as much guides for me as I am for them. It's a challenging journey, but I wouldn't trade it for anything in the cosmos. Becoming a mother made me better, more resilient, and dare I say gave me a new lens with which to view some of my own mom's struggles. When you are cut open for your children to have life and have to learn to be mobile again while in excruciating pain, it humbles you. My mom was there to help me to the bathroom, bathe me, and help me get my mobility back. So, however imperfect I have found her style of parenting, I'd like to think we were gifted those moments to illustrate the perfection in full circle moments and cycles of life.

If we take notice, motherhood allows us and our bloodlines to surrender to transformation and healing. I look forward to watching my kids perfect what I give them in their own way. It's not an affront to what I offered them as a mother. We should want to see the next generation not only succeed, but to become more aligned, happy, and whole as humans (and not by conventional societal standards either). We ought to be championing the next generation to eradicate generational trauma and familial distortions.

> ***Evolving Soul Reflection:*** *Motherhood and parenthood, in general, shows up differently for every person. Whether your road was difficult or filled with loving memories, it is an experience worthy of unpacking to glean the necessary wisdom. Choosing to bring life into this world is both courageous and admirable. Honor where you are on your journey and abandon the notion that there is a specific way of doing this right. Remember that you too are a child growing up. Be gentle with yourself.*
>
> *Time to do some reflecting evolving souls. What kind of relationship do you have with your mother? What are some ways that relationship comes up for you? Even if you aren't a parent to a child, we all reach a place where we must re-parent ourselves based on our upbringing and experiences. What attributes are important to you in a parent and why? Jot down ways that you can embody those characteristics so you can show up for yourself in those ways.*

Use the space below to document your evolving soul reflections. Hugging you from a distance.

WHEN I
CLOSE MY
EYES,
ALL I SEE IS
WEALTH
AND
PROMINENCE.

"SOMETIMES LOVE ISN'T ENOUGH"

January 31st, 2019

My current truth and realization is that you can't love away a person's demons. Sometimes you love and love and give so much to another that you deplete yourself. Not everyone is ready for what you have to offer, and that narrative doesn't change whether you are married or randomly dating. It doesn't diminish the offering or who you are, it just means the person you may want to give your all to isn't the rightful receiver of your affections and all-spark. We never lose when we love another, but the lessons hurt, and the healing is often dark. Self-sabotage is a real thing. It doesn't just show up in the person who won't receive the gift of your love, but it is inherent in you because you won't let go enough to allow the right thing to show up for you.

You can be the best partner/spouse/companion, provide a happy home, and do all the "right" things. None of it matters when the person you are doing it for isn't ready for you or can't appreciate the offering. When this happens, you learn that no matter how great the love, you must always choose yourself. As humans, unfortunately, we respond with the entitlement of immediacy or only see the necessity of change when we lose something dear. Don't let that thing you lose be yourself.

> **Evolving Soul Reflection:** *I've learned that it isn't my job to coax anyone to love me. You either love me or you don't. It's also not my job to fix or heal people. Everyone must go on their own journey to awakening as I did to find the answers and heal themselves. I am merely here to illuminate the path through how I live my life, and as it best suits me. The same is true for you. You are a powerful illuminator of paths. Love yourself. Protect yourself and appreciate yourself. My Dad always said you teach people how to treat you. In the words of Jay-Z, tell those who want to be in your life to either "love you or leave you alone."*
>
> *Time to do some journaling, evolving souls. Reflect upon the relationships in your life both platonic and romantic. What are those instances where your love wasn't reciprocated? What did you learn about yourself and what to do differently in the future?*

Use the space below to document your evolving soul reflections. You can never go wrong with choosing yourself.

LOVE IS A HELLUVA DRUG

I'm a sucker for love. I think I always have been. Looking at the romantic relationships around me, there was little to inspire but a lot to detract me from traveling down similar paths to love or operating in some of the ways I observed growing up. My first love was different. Very much unlike my dad, rebellious in a delicious way, coming from a family quite a bit different from mine. I liked it that way. It wasn't that my dad wasn't someone to emulate, or even someone I lacked admiration for. There had just been too many stories of dysfunctional love spawned from the lives of my dad's underdeveloped and misogynist peer group as well as family members who were quite obviously clueless about love and what it took to cultivate a healthy relationship romantically. I wanted to open myself to something different.

"DeShawn" was something else and together we were something to behold. We liked the same music, were crazy stylish, and had a soul connection at that age that defied both of our senses. Like most young love, age and a desperate desire to be adored, chosen, and loved led a woefully inexperienced, younger Janine down a rabbit hole of deception, hurt, and mindsets that would set me up for at least two decades of misconceptions and unfortunate lessons in life and love.

It took me seventeen years to realize that every piece of advice I was given as an adolescent and every word "De-shawn" projected upon me was the foundation upon which I built my persona as a girlfriend and eventually a wife. It stung to see how a time so far in the rearview led me down such a wayward path of accepting less than I ever deserved and had me overcompensating for a man who was incapable and unwilling to grow in love with me.

When adults say young people are "impressionable" it isn't all the way wrong, but it needs some refining. Instead, I would say unevolved people are "impressionable." I was impressionable when my young age aligned with my lack of life experience would suggest I should have known better. No matter how mature you think you are in actuality or in your head, there will always be gaps in how you see things until you garner a variety of experiences. Something as silly as "De-Shawn" saying that I never spent money on him or on our dates led me to gravitate toward total independence, ensuring that the next man that entered my life knew that I could split a bill or pay one with no issue. Hearing from my parents ad nauseam about how independence was imperative further cemented the notion that I needed to not only have my own money, but that I couldn't count on relaxing into my femininity and being courted by a man. My shift in behavior was also enduring, as that next man also got accustomed to us sharing everything financially and lacked the will to be a true provider and the chivalrous temperament to wine and dine me in the years to come. I couldn't see it because I was too busy propping myself up on being the down-to-earth woman who didn't need much to be happy in a relationship. The foolishness!

It is incredibly dangerous to be creating your persona based on what will be accepted by others. Worst yet, it is destructive to lower your own evolution to meet the slow crawl of another in the name of love. Love will meet you where you are at. If you don't know your self-worth, it will meet you there. If you settle in love, it will meet you there. If you don't love yourself enough to honor what will truly make you happy, it will meet you there. Each time, it will be a new, yet familiar character that will love you to the degree you are able to honor yourself.

Regardless of your gender or sexual preference, you ought to learn to be with yourself and love yourself before you start contriving a version of yourself for another to be loved. Until you love yourself, you will undoubtedly attract characters who suffer with various levels of self-hatred and inauthenticity in both your platonic and romantic relationships. The lessons can be enduring and painful if you are seeking validation from people who, like you, are still figuring out which character they will play in the screenplay of life. Be aware of who and where you are deriving your examples of love from. The beauty about experience is that we get to take what resonates while leaving the rest behind. Your experience is the content with which you get to map your life. Be honest about what you truly desire and do the work to become that which you seek. Don't settle until your life in love and otherwise becomes a reflection of all that you embody on the inside.

Use the space below to document your evolving soul reflections. Who or what informs how you show up in your romantic relationships? What needs to shift for you to have more fulfilling relationships in love?

EVERY THORN THAT HAS PIERCED MY CROWN AND MY HEART LET LIGHT IN. MY WOUNDS GREW FLOWERS.

DANGEROUS MINDS

Following my first love, there were short-lived attractions that played out and fizzled out in their divine time, but there is one that would be a twenty-year lesson of epic proportions.

What is the outcome when you're seventeen years old and possess the capability of learning from prior mistakes by shifting your behaviors and mindsets? As I shared already, it took me almost two decades to recall how I could have both created and fallen prey to the man I married, but when I sifted through the archives, the answer was there and I wasn't pleased. I wasn't pleased with "DeShawn" who I suspect planted these rogue seeds within me from a place of inexperience and his own wayward upbringing which sprouted into a healthy helping of unfavorable behaviors. I was even more displeased with my then husband who had knowingly, cleverly, and comfortably feasted on that version of me, but more importantly, I was mad at myself for normalizing treatment that was clearly beneath me.

Let me demonstrate how innocence coupled with your upbringing and coming of age can set the course for your life in wayward ways. Again, I was seventeen years old, an old soul, and by most of my peers' account and even adults who encountered me an extremely mature seventeen-year-old. By comparison to where I sit currently, which is in my late thirties, all my maturity at seventeen had not yet provided me with enough lived experience to understand the myriad of ways my decisions could impact the direction of my life.

In comes "Venom Pain," a known entity in school for his good looks, charismatic demeanor, and adjacency to the cool kids in school. I first encountered him in junior high school while walking home with friends. He was two years older, but I remember walking home with my girlfriends and him and his boys bothering them. I thought he was annoying at first, but eventually I started to wish he would bother me a bit too. Be careful what you wish for, ladies! I have no concrete recollection of how much thought I had given to the possibility that he may shift his interest to bugging me, but he eventually did. I loved it and hated it all at once.

Once I eventually made it to high school, I would run into him from time to time. The interactions were more mature and pleasant. I was with "DeShawn" for 9th and 10th grade, and I watched "Venom Pain" date a girl or two. Once "DeShawn" and I parted ways, I was tipped off that "Venom Pain" wanted to date me. We spoke a few times on the phone, and I let him know I was keeping my options open by getting to know a few other boys. He gave an ultimatum that I am sure would be deemed a red flag by most young women today, and it was that I had to make a choice between him and the other guy I was talking to at the time. I chose the other guy and we parted on friendly terms. I'm not going to BS you, the guy I chose was twenty-three, intelligent, and easy on the eyes. His Bajan background made him that much more of a catch in my eyes at the time. It was all good until he ended up in county jail.

I don't have to explain the mathematics of how a daughter of an NYPD Sergeant doesn't exactly compute with a felon, so that fizzled expeditiously. In similar fashion, I am not so sure the daughter of an NYPD Sergeant belongs co-mingling with the son of a man who was incarcerated in Sing Sing for repeated egregious crimes. Fast forward through the granules of my teenage decisions, "Venom Pain" and I ended up together, and it felt like magic. He was quiet, he had the same disdain for our classmates and high school life that I did, he had a reverence for the cosmos, and genuinely seemed to enjoy my company. In retrospect, I think part of what bonded us was how easy it was to be with one another; we found peace just being together, but more importantly, we were both trying to escape our respective family lives for different reasons. Our many young adult days together blossomed quickly into trips out of the country, solidifying our careers, moving in together, and eventually getting married and having kids.

To hear others tell it, we were the example others looked to in terms of a romantic couple. We became the example of enduring love and our kids the product of a loving partnership started when we were just kids. There was no question throughout and even with more clarity today that the "Venom Pain" was a troubled person. Both of his biological parents had successfully gotten him to planet Earth, but not much longer after his birth had been victims of addiction and willing participants in illegal behaviors. With that, he was raised by his mom's sister and her husband from the time he was ten months old. I struggled early in our relationship to find common ground between what his family and mine represented. This was the first time in my life that I had been faced with so much chaos and destruction within a family via the legal system and addiction. His aunt had become the Mother Hale and matriarch of the family caring for anyone and everyone who fell sick or had been left abandoned. I guess I never spent enough time evaluating what that does to a person and how it might inform their relationships in the future. All I ever saw was a loving person who had an unfortunate yet fortunate upbringing, and I figured if I could show him what life could be like, if perhaps we created a wholly new life together, it may make the difference.

One of my meditation instructors said that the mind is a dangerous place. I remember hearing it and thinking, this is the damn truth! I spent years trying to understand the private mental and emotional space of the "Venom Pain." He wasn't much for sharing and this became a deficit in our relationship as I craved more depth with him. For years, I would request more openness, more depth; I had even expressed it in tears. I would get in return, "Don't cry, I will change."

I watched how he was when he would speak to his aunt. He was endearing, yes, but when she would assuredly belt out "I love you" at the end of the conversation, it often lacked in tone as much as it did in authenticity. Love was a foreign concept for him, as he so often proclaimed. He claimed he had no example of love since his parents weren't around and he was raised by his aunt and uncle. I was dedicated to being a good wife and loving him where he was, despite the ways his lack of affection and love were eating away at me. Top this off with our consistent financial woes, which had my house in pre-foreclosure twice and household expenses eating away at the early gains in my business, and you have quite literally a volcano prepping for eruption.

I set the precedent from our dating days that I was not only willing to pull my weight financially, but I was capable. I think we can all agree that despite our new age proclamations of what a woman can bring to the table, there is nothing sexier than a man who ensures the safety and stability of the family both physically and financially. If your setup or outlook is different on this, that is perfectly fine. Don't shoot the messenger. I'm merely suggesting that beyond traditional societal gender roles, there is something within healthy masculine energy that has a devout need to protect and provide and healthy feminine energy to nurture and create. "Venom Pain" lacked in the "protect and provide" aspect of masculinity, especially as he was fortunate to have a partner within me that was high-achieving and could make more than a few bucks outside of the confines of Corporate Amerikkka. I have no problem saying it with my chest that I was worthy of being taken care of in every way. It never happened the way it should have, for which I am thankful on my best days and still disgusted on my petty days. I'm human.

Imagine going out to dinner with your husband and he turns to ask you if there is enough in the joint account for it. This was most of our dinners out. A stark contrast from my upbringing with a father who never looked to my mother for those things ever, but somehow, I had strayed far from that lesson. He is an NYPD Detective. Somewhat consciously and certainly unconsciously, I knew there was something wrong that the money never seemed to add up or afford our family with the comfort that we desired and deserved. Here I was circa 2012, two children in, my business and my image coming into prominence and yet at home I was living a vastly different life that didn't feel fair or natural in the name of family and love.

The first time I went to re-modify our mortgage, I had to compile all our financials. It was the first time I started to wonder who I was married to. In looking at his bank statements, he had been spending not hundreds but thousands of our dollars on treats for himself, dinners, etc. This is after he would console me through tears and dread as I saw the fruits of my labor via Talent Think Innovations go up in smoke because I was constantly padding our household financial deficits with my revenue. He apologized for mismanaging our money and insisted things would get better, but ultimately there were more outputs to our money than he was willing to come clean about at that time. As my Grandma Marie would always say, "what you do in the dark, would always come to light."

In October 2015, I went to a makeup influencers event in NYC with my then best friend, Melissa. I was mostly there to support her putting her talents out there as a makeup artist. There were up-and-coming influencers in beauty and lifestyle in the building doing everything from meet and greets to informational panels. During our day-sipping and knowledge gathering we happened upon two psychics. At that time, I was vehemently against psychics as one of my grandmothers had seen one decades before who had predicted some unfortunate family events. Plainly, the knowledge of the unbridled truth of things and predictions of the future scared me. Still, my friend was kind of this free-wielding Gemini who saw the psychics as an opportunity for us to do something adventurous together. I said no indignantly, but she begged. My compromise was that she goes first. If she felt like they were legit, I would consider doing it. Less than five minutes into her sitting with the psychic, she began to cry and said, "Neen, please do it. She is spot on." I was shook, but I made her a promise. I decided to get a reading. The psychic sat with me and read me for filth. She told me that I was content but not happy in my marriage, and that I would be the one to end it. She told me some other things about people I couldn't trust around me any longer, but this part about me ending my marriage pierced my soul and sent me into a state of terror.

My friend and I were so shaken by the truth of what we were told, we found ourselves holding hands at the bar and praying. I struggled with how to broach the topic of a potential divorce with "Venom Pain," but in my gut I had to say something. What I shared may surprise you.

When I went home, he asked how the event was and I told him it was great. I shared with him that I had gotten coerced into sitting with a psychic. Since I couldn't bring myself to say what she told me, I told him instead that she said he was cheating on me and would eventually divorce me. This statement becomes important the deeper we go in this story because it had a purpose. He quickly assuaged my fears by letting me know that he would never divorce me and that it wasn't true. Still, there was something about the experience that gnawed at me. It would be another two years before I would know exactly why.

2017 marked our 10-year wedding anniversary and a total of 17 years together. That year, I felt we were more or less in a good place, and I wanted to commemorate our love and devotion to one another. This is when I set out on a quest for us to renew our vows. He agreed it would be a nice thing to do. We were three kids into our relationship and had weathered many hurdles to reach that point. That May, I managed to throw a beautiful, intimate dinner with our family to celebrate our wedding anniversary, but trying to organize a vow renewal ceremony was proving to be impossible. No matter where I looked or what I tried to organize it wasn't coming together. Feeling somewhat defeated, I abandoned the whole idea and opted for us to take a family trip to St. Thomas with my mom and our kids. Everything that could have gone wrong both before the trip and during did. Nevertheless, we went on to enjoy a lovely time away.

August 10th, 2017 was a Thursday and I now know it was also the 222nd day of that year. My mystic folks will understand why that number is significant. That aside, I sauntered down to our basement to look for an old photo of myself to post for throwback Thursday, but instead I started thumbing through some pictures he had from trips to Cancun, Mexico. I quickly got bored with the pictures as I had seen them many times over, so I moved on to looking for my picture. Once I found a picture I wanted to post, I put the envelope of pictures back and closed the Rubbermaid bin that we kept all our pictures in. As I walked away, I heard loudly in my head, "go back!" I slightly ignored it and then I heard it again. The voice said, "go back and pull the negatives!" I didn't hesitate this time and I went back to the pictures I was thumbing through to find the negatives. There were three negative sheets. I took the first one and held it up to this uncovered lightbulb that served as the lighting for our basement and looked at each frame carefully. Before I even looked carefully at the negatives my stomach got sour and dropped. There were several pictures that had been omitted from what was developed. These pictures showed "Venom Pain" hugged up and tightly holding multiple women in different frames in ways he had yet to embrace me. What immediately struck me was the posturing and essence coming from each subsequent frame. The man I was observing looked to be comfortable in these pictures with these unknown women. You would have never known he was a married man, because there was a freedom and joy about him. I didn't know the man I was observing, and in some crazy way I slightly wished I knew this particular version of him because he was giving more flavor in those negatives than he had ever attempted to give me. It is worth noting that this trip happened in 2009, a mere few months after I gave birth to our first child together. I wasn't hype about this trip, but I also was never a woman to tell another human what they could or could not do.

After the initial shock and snapping of what felt like a branch in my mind, I called him and asked him to remind me of the years he went to Cancun. Like a champ, he verified for me when it was and I knew I had enough ammo to discuss the matter with him. What was extraordinary to me was my level of calm. You would have thought that I would have chosen violence, but really, when I approached the bench, I came with more questions than chaotic proclamations.

I simply asked him to help me understand what all was going on in Mexico when he went and how he found himself so cozy and familiar with several women pictured. He, of course, denied any wrongdoing at first, but when I asked him to cut on the light and see what I saw, it was then that the story switched up. His claim was that the women in the picture were random people he and his trash ass best friend encountered while out and about. According to his account, they never slept with any of them, and it was all just pictures. It was at that moment that I let him know I had genuinely and generously given him 17 years of my life and that I would not be giving him another 17 years like that again. I quite confidently proclaimed that I would be focusing on myself going forward and that he needed to figure out his life and what he wanted to do.

That month it had seemed a few men I knew had lost their minds. My best friend at the time was going through it with her husband, as was her mom. In hindsight, the prismatic reflection of my relationship and theirs taking a nose-dive was interesting to witness all at once. Nonetheless, I remember speaking with my friend at the time about an old schoolmate of ours who had always kept in touch and who we both knew had a deep reverence for me. I told her I was now considering meeting up with him after years of intentionally blowing him off. She encouraged me to go for it and that was all I needed to hear. I reached out to him via Instagram and let him know we could meet up. He had been one of my very best friends, and I let go of him to be the consummate girlfriend and later wife. I saw no reason why I should isolate myself in that way any more, and so I didn't. A new version of myself was underway.

You see, "being good," "perfection," and "martyr-like" behavior is actually a result of conditioning and oftentimes trauma. It is also extremely circumstantial and transient. Meaning you can only be as good as the circumstances and timing of things will allow. In my life, there came a point where forcing myself to adhere to the "good wife" archetype was slipping from my fingers like fine grains of sand, because everything around me was conspiring to awaken me to other untapped aspects of myself. Pretty soon after this discovery, I realized I had done well to solidify my professional identity, but somewhere along the journey I had forgotten who "Janine Nicole" was in the name of love and that was no longer fine with me.

For a few months, we tried to mend the relationship. In hindsight, I'm not sure how much of an active participant I was. That fall, I had taken a trip to my GYN only to get that dreaded call that my pap smear came back abnormal. In over 20 years of me seeing a GYN, I had never received that call. Naturally, I went to "Venom Pain" with questions. He had no answers and seemed rather unaffected by my terror. It would be six months before I could test again. Full disclosure, this abnormal pap smear test did not conclude I had an STD or STI, but what was found could have been a precursor to that being true. Nonetheless, I did everything in my power to ensure the next pap was pristine. The only way to ensure that would happen was to stop being intimate with "Venom Pain." When you get married, the assumption is that you are safe to be with your husband, without protection, and all will be well. In my case, the abnormal pap smear was a smoke signal of bigger issues in my marriage, and whoever looks over me from the realms was not about to have me go out like that.

I am happy to share that in April 2018, I got retested and everything was fine, proving my former point. "Venom Pain" became increasingly strange and different as I became more liberated and detached from him both mentally and emotionally. By this time, I had told him that he was free from feeling any obligation to love me or care for me in that way. At this point, our relationship had been reduced to the business of our kids and our home. We were operating more as roommates than husband and wife. While love had fizzled between him and me, it was bubbling over between my schoolmate and me.

That previous November of 2017, I did exactly what I said I would and met up with my old friend. I remember feeling nervous about it and chatting with a business colleague about it during our meeting. She was an older woman and so I appreciated her take on it all. I remember her asking me, "why are you feeling so anxious to see this guy? Is it because you think you may feel something for him?" I sheepishly smiled and said maybe. She said and so what if you do? What does that mean? She said you both are grown and there is no reason two friends can't meet up for drinks. She was right, and this was the first time that I understood the statement that "feelings are not facts." We have a gazillion feelings every day. Why was I concerned about anything that might come up for me after seeing this gentleman?

I made sure our time together was short yet purposeful. When I texted him that I was still up for the meeting, he was in shock. We met up for about an hour before I had to go to see my grandmother in Queens and it was wonderful. We caught up, had some drinks, laughed, and genuinely enjoyed our time together. Even today, I don't believe either of us had any intention of carrying on anything beyond that day, but what happened next was the game changer.

This schoolmate, who shall be known as "Dr. Medley" from this point on, asked if he could walk me to my car. I thought it was a nice gesture, so I agreed. We walked and talked for a bit until we reached the lane my car was in. I turned to him and told him it was nice to see him again and catch up. He asked if he could have a hug and so we did. As we hugged, it seemed neither of us wanted to let go and in return, I spoke aloud an "oh God." He asked me what was wrong, and I said, "nothing, I'm fine." I wanted to kiss him, but I didn't want to cross that line, so I kissed him gently on his cheek and told him to be well. I got in my car and let out a bunch of consecutive curses, but also couldn't stop smiling. Unbeknownst to me, he would circle back to my window and knock on it. I rolled it down and he said, "can I get another of those kisses?" I kissed him on his cheek again and said goodbye. I never had any intentions of letting him know what I felt. I was going to ride out to my grandmother's house and let it live in the annals of my mind. As I was driving to Queens, he texted me saying, "I know you are driving, so please don't text back right now, but let me know when you get to Queens safely." He went on to say that he "had never had a hug like that and that we needed to discuss our encounter." From this day on, my relationship with "Venom Pain" and quite frankly my life was never the same in the best way possible. My life wasn't simply better because "Dr. Medley" and I ended up in this secret love affair. That ended up being a saga within a saga in the end. My life was better, because the encounter birthed a new me in many different versions over the course of three years leading me to uncover all I needed to know about "Venom Pain" to end our toxic marriage and eventually preparing me for the entrance of the one I had been waiting for my entire life, my universal gift, my king, Terrence L. Williams, no alias required.

You may be thinking what in the Jada Pinkett-Smith kind of entanglement is this, and maybe you're right. I think I see it somewhat differently and perhaps you may as you understand more once you learn more about "Venom Pain's" actions. By the Spring of 2018, I was rocking and rolling professionally. I had bookings for me to speak in many states through December. Talent Think Innovations was hot! I also was looking at a surgery to repair an umbilical hernia at the end of May. The morning I went in for surgery, I was polishing up a final draft of a whitepaper for a client. "Venom Pain" drove me to my surgery and stayed throughout, but it would be a few years before I recognized how little he tended to my care immediately thereafter. That was all divinely orchestrated because it was my younger brother who I ended up calling up to help me during my recovery with the kids, house, etc. It was also a crucial time in our siblingship, coming off of a few rough years of disconnection and resentment. It was an absolute moment in time in which I was able to confide in him about what was happening in my marriage. He let me know then that he was leery of "Venom Pain" and how he operated with me given my accomplishments and professional status. It felt like a relief to have him as my confidante and to have him affirm what I was experiencing. Little did I know, he would also be the one to help me discover the last of the missing pieces to "Venom Pain's" infidelity another two years later during the pandemic.

The Summer of 2018, we took what was our final family vacation. I distinctly recall this one discussion we were having driving from Pompano Beach, Florida to his family's home in Palm Bay, where he plainly let me know that no man would want me with three kids. I went on to offer him the many examples of girlfriends and acquaintances I knew of who went into their respective relationships with two or more kids and blended their families beautifully. He dug in deeper on his point, and eventually we abandoned the discussion. I remember feeling motivated and excited about where I would land beyond him so he could eat crow. Thankfully, he went back home shortly thereafter, and the kids and I stayed behind to spend some additional time with my prima, Lauren. The additional two weeks was precisely what I needed to clear my head and decide what my next steps would be.

By September of 2018, my connection with "Dr. Medley" had deepened further. One night, "Venom Pain" came home and asked if we could speak. I sat down at our kitchen table, and he said, "I didn't want it to come to this, but you were right; I do see you as a mother figure and not a wife." He went on to add that he couldn't love me the way I deserved to be loved and that I should go find my vibe. To give you a visual, he did this with bloodshot eyes and tears running down his face. More so than having empathy for his tears, I felt relief and a universal wink that I was now free to live. I spent the time after his proclamation consoling him, which speaks so much to how much more work I needed to do on myself. Truly, how was I consoling someone who was intentionally harming me? In fairness, that lasted that night and not a day beyond that time. By the next day, I had bigger questions for him about the direction of our relationship. I asked him if he was trying to divorce me, and his answer was "no." I was perplexed. I asked him what he ultimately wanted; he said he didn't know exactly. I left it alone and told him that I had supported his professional pursuits all of these years and now it is time for him to support me in any way I needed him to without question. I told him I reserved the right to divorce him if our living situation became intolerable to me. He agreed to my terms. In the coming weeks, I would ask more pointed questions of him as to what the rules of engagement were now that he was sending me to find love with other men. I wanted to hear him tell me what he envisioned, because I knew what I was prepared to do. Could I date with his knowledge? Was sex with others reasonable or not? Did he have some sort of finite timeline in sight for when this would all end? These were all questions I was interested in him answering. Although he had cried a river in September, my line of questioning had brought about a much more serious reality that I wasn't about to let him run me into the ground with his warped vision for our marriage and he now understood that I, too, was happy to go find out what made me happy as he had suggested I do.

The end of 2018 left me somewhere between this world and the celestial skies mentally. I was neither here nor there. I wrapped a healthy year of work and was excited for 2019 as I would start my journey in the wellness space as a Mindfulness Meditation Instructor. Professionally, everything was amazing, but my love life was fast becoming one of those 1,000-piece puzzles. Dr. Medley had disappeared in November of 2018 without a trace, and I was feeling dissatisfied with what I was getting in both directions, yet excited about the freedom to discover what I needed in love as an adult. Something needed to change quickly, and I was motivated to make the necessary adjustments.

Even through my pain towards the end of 2018, I decided what 2019 was going to be. It was going to be what I called my

"Year of Hedonism and Exploration." I had already come to the conclusion that I would actually be financially better off without Venom. The majority of the debts that were crippling us were his, with the only outlier being our house. I was motivated to shed every aspect of my life that kept me attached to him and further off my path.

At the top of 2019, I booked a former tarot reader, Nailea Guererro, for a love tarot reading. I wanted to do a pulse check to see if I was on the right path. During the reading, divorce immediately came up. She asked me why I would continue to put it off? Deception was also rampant in the reading. Her advice to me at the time was I needed to start to prioritize my happiness. She went on to tell me that happy kids will stem from a happy mommy. It was then that I started researching divorce mediators in our area and let "Venom Pain" know I was not happy with how things were. I distinctly remember asking him how he felt about the state of our relationship and his response was, "I'm good." If 2018 marked the beginning of his bizarre behavior, 2019 was peak bizarre. It was the year I became repulsed by him. By this time, our relationship was wide open in that I was living my life as if single and he was operating as his usual self since he had very clearly been doing whatever and whoever his loins led him to our entire relationship. We would still have occasional amicable discussions. I specifically recall this one discussion in early March surrounding my trip to a soft play party where I was going to learn more about tantric sex. After months and months of him basically operating with me as if a roommate, it was as if I piqued his interest with my attendance of this event. The day after I attended, I woke up to him in my face to which I asked why he was so close to me. He stated that he missed his "Janineenie-weenie/choonks" which were his two nicknames for me. I looked at him both puzzled and annoyed, and said, "what do you mean?" He went on to say he wanted to hear about my time at the play party. All I could remember thinking is that this is strange and not right to have your husband excited to hear about your night which entailed time spent with another man. I realized I was finally speaking his language as this was, in his head, equal to his zeal for all things sex and perversion. I felt no compulsion to share any of the nitty gritty details with him about my night. I just kept asking him why he wanted to know. He replied, "Because it sounded interesting." The greatest satisfaction of that night was knowing that I had connected with a man we will call "The Master Teacher" that embodied a divinity that far exceeded what I was experiencing with Venom. "The Master Teacher" was gentle, attentive, and as connected to the cosmos as I was. To this day, the squad and I have a great deal of reverence for the lessons he imparted on us via our short-lived connection. It was delicious to know that Venom thought I was just out here sharing myself sexually with men the way he was with women for our entire relationship. The reality was I wasn't. I was exploring my ability to attract the divinity within me. This became my compass that would eventually let me know how close I was to truly having the love my heart desired come into my life.

March of 2019 marked my first international solo trip to Seville, Spain. This trip was life-changing because it was the first time I had been to Spain, a place I had learned about throughout high school and college and had a deep love for. Maybe a week before my trip, I was packing and Venom had the audacity to ask me if I felt some sort of way that we wouldn't be experiencing Spain together; my answer was "no." He replied, "I knew you would say that." Although Spain was meant to be a solo endeavor, I met and connected with so much soul family while away that it all just reinforced how little I needed his energy in my life any more.

By April of 2019, we had met with divorce mediators to start to plan what going our separate ways would look like. We had opted for a more civil divorce than duking it out in court and wasting precious energy and money. There was still a softness to me at this point. I remember sitting with the mediators that were comprised of a husband-and-wife duo. The wife was a counselor of sorts, and the husband was the attorney. The wife had questioned me on why I was avoiding a more solid and perhaps stringent parenting plan. She warned that things start amicable in mediation, but life moves on and people get into new relationships among other things. I took the advice even though in my mind I was secretly hoping we would come to an agreement that felt like an easy transition for our kids. I learned eventually that the wife couldn't have been more right. In the end, I had to develop that stringent parenting plan and so much more.

To further prove my point that things in my life are incredibly synchronistic, I will share how I came by my divorce attorney. A girlfriend of mine had invited a few friends out to this wonderful lounge in Brooklyn called Bembe. While I was sure I was going out that night for dancing, great drinks, and to lose myself in world music, I landed myself the attorney that would free me from this toxic marriage. As I walked into the venue, on a Monday no less, I saw my friend with a few other women sitting at a table. As I greeted everyone and sat down, one of the women was discussing her own marital problems and disaster of a divorce. I listened intently, thinking, how is this the conversation right now? One of the other women spoke up and said I'm a divorce attorney and continued to give some advice. My girlfriend, Cash, nudged me and said is it okay for me to share your situation. I was like "hell yeah." Once I started to detail what was going on and the steps I had taken, the divorce attorney said, how much are those mediators charging you? I told her the price to which she responded, "I can get your divorce finalized for half that rate." My heart leapt with thanks. I asked her for her number, and we went on to party the night away epically.

The next day I texted her to start the conversation. After a few false starts due to Venom not keeping up his end of the bargain by paying half of her fees, I finally retained her in July of 2019. His bizarre, destructive, and elusive behavior continued throughout 2019. After a few iterations to our initial divorce stipulation, it was finally filed on October 25th, 2019. A date that hadn't meant much to me upon seeing it until I met my king, Terrence. His birthday happens to be October 25th. Let that marinate.

By November of 2019, I served him papers. Part of the reason things took so long to be filed was because I didn't want him to be served at work and have to be faced with a lot of questions. There were a few additional steps required for me to be able to serve him in our home unbeknownst to him. For months leading up to this point, there was a smug demeanor about him. It was almost as if he thought I was bluffing about divorcing him. Truthfully, I hadn't spoken about the countless conversations I had with Helen or the plan. The goal was simply to deliver. When I served him, I offered him a little over a week to review and come back to me with any concerns. Four days into that week, I was awakened by him saying he wanted to talk about the divorce. This brilliant conversation he wanted to have with me went like this:

Venom: "Hey...I've been reading the divorce papers, and I was thinking about how you will be without benefits. I'm worried about you, and I don't want anything to happen to you, so how about we postpone the divorce proceedings so you can stay on my benefits and get a separation instead? When I retire in a few years and both of us have more money, we can go through with the divorce then."

Please take a moment to envision me being awakened out of a good sleep to this incredibly manipulative conversation. Sidebar: Yes, shamefully, I was still sleeping in bed with this joker at the time; I have no redeeming words for this. All I remember is I perked up rather quickly, rubbed my eyes, and sat up straight to make sure I heard his proposition clearly.

My stomach immediately became sour at the notion of spending any more years with him than I already had. I said to him, "the mere notion of this being prolonged any further makes me sick. I have already envisioned a new life for myself, and it doesn't include rolling back our divorce filing." As far as my health insurance, I thanked him for his "concern" and assured him I had done my research on options for health coverage. What you have to appreciate here is that he had already wasted 17 years of my life with his nonsense. The proposition was not at all about preserving my well-being through his health coverage, otherwise he might have moved differently all throughout our relationship, but instead he posed harm to my health on more than one occasion. If you really examine what he said, his chief concern was not my well-being, but his own. He was concerned about the financial toll it would take on him in the present and was hoping that I would let him get to retirement whereby either I would find I didn't want to divorce him, or he would have more money to be divorced. I must note here that it was a prevailing theory of his that perhaps all we needed was a break and that perhaps we would remarry one another after being apart. If I ever questioned whether he had learned anything about me in 17 years, it was in moments like this that it became glaring he didn't know me at all. There is no gradience in my interest in a person. I am either all in or you don't exist to me. The idea that he would set me free to potentially commingle and connect among the 8 billion people walking planet Earth and still choose him is arrogant and laughable. Every business trip I have ever taken or conference I have ever spoken at has been chock full of eligible bachelors who have tried their way with me to no avail. Options were never my issue, he was.

That conversation went nowhere and resulted in me getting him to agree to sign the papers at his earliest convenience. That November, I had been served some papers as well. I was served pre-foreclosure paperwork right before the holidays letting me know I may lose my home. He was handling our mortgage at the time. When I asked him how this could be, he said "you told me to hold off on the mortgage in the Summer." Delaying a payment was never a directive to not pay at all for months, but this was his typical modus operandi of making sure he wasn't the only one left righting the wrongs. Once more, I had to pick up the pieces and lawyer up to ensure we didn't lose our home. Let me tell you about my family. When I shared what was going on and what I was having to manage before the holiday, they said, "listen, you're never going to be homeless, we won't let it happen ever...you're going to be fine, the kids will be fine." It was at that moment that I let go of any fears I had surrounding my home. I worked the process and system and eventually I was able to get it re-modified and listed for sale.

By this time now, I had also decided that I would be moving out of our home by summer of 2020 and eventually out of state with our kids. I was leaning heavily towards North Carolina, as I had grown to love it quite a bit while taking weekend trips to visit with friends throughout the previous two years. With everything falling apart and yet together at home, I wanted to get away for NYE 2019 and be with people who loved me, so the kids and I took a road trip to North Carolina. I had discussed the prospect of this trip with Venom months prior and he agreed it was fine. As we got closer, I asked him if he wanted to contribute financially towards the trip via paying some of the Airbnb fees. He responded, "I would have thought you would have canceled the trip with everything we have going on." To illustrate how little the ask was, we were staying in three different states over the course of a week. I had already covered all of our hotel stays, Airbnb deposit, and spending money. He was only being asked to cover about $180 plus dollars. I would find out in 2020 exactly why this was a hard ask, but at the time, I shrugged it off and covered it all. I packed and shuffled off at 3am on the morning of December 27th en route to Virginia, our first stop on the way to North Carolina. As the kids got settled in my truck and I started to map my bearings, Venom said goodbye to the kids and then motions for me to lower my window. He goes on to say, "I know we're divorcing, but we're not enemies. You can hug me you know." I got out of the car begrudgingly and awkwardly leaned into a half hug.

The kids and I went on to have a wonderful time on our trip. Upon getting to our Airbnb in Cary, North Carolina, we opened the front door to see prisms of rainbows everywhere. They were on the couch, the kitchen counter, and the floor. I knew that leaving Venom where he was for a place I might settle with my kids was the right decision to have made. Our time in North Carolina was so restorative that by the time we were set to leave Baltimore on the way back, I opted to stay for an additional two days to avoid coming home to him.

Upon returning home to NY in January 2020, I had come to many conclusions, but one that needed immediate attention. That was the matter of us sleeping in the same bed. As I said, shamefully, that went on longer than I believe I should have allowed. I had bought a long body pillow which I kept between us, so I didn't have to feel even an appendage touching my skin. I would tuck my covers in so he couldn't try to weasel in, and trust me, he tried on more than one occasion leading me to purchase a blanket from the kids for him for Christmas 2019 so he would leave me alone. For the record, I have never understood this concept of being in a divorce proceeding and still being intimate. My parents did it, and my father had normalized sex during that time as "available and familiar." I, on the other hand, felt it was a gross contradiction with the action we were taking to separate. Giving of myself to Venom sexually had long ended as you have read, but it was to the point that I wanted him not to touch me in any manner.

One night in January of 2020, I was sharing with a few of my girlfriends known as "The Namigas" that I couldn't stomach him let alone continue sharing a bed and that I was going to move into our fourth bedroom/my office effective immediately. They said, "say less, what size bed do you want?" Each of them started screenshotting pictures of inflatable mattresses into the chat and I settled on one. Several cash transfers later and they sent me the confirmation from Amazon that my new bed was on its way. For me, this was another huge step of severing ties from him, and it felt great.

The day the bed came, and I grabbed my pillows and covers to go downstairs, Venom's response was, "you don't want to sleep with me any more?" There is a popular word used for men like Venom who are on the surface charismatic and charming but use it to manipulate and gas-light their partners. I will refrain from using it here, but if you know, you know. Taking more space from him meant he would find new ways of invading my space, like using the bathroom while I was brushing my teeth or brushing past me so that I could feel his soft dick on my ass as if that could ignite something dormant in me. These things amidst his growing concerns and panic about what divorce would mean for him were the gripes and wars fought in February 2020.

At this juncture, I was praying my lawyer Helen was right, and that we were maybe 2–3 months from receiving a judgment on our divorce. That was until the world slowed its spin and the pandemic came rolling in. As most humans did, it became annoyingly real that I was literally having to hunker down with the man I was trying to create more space from. He became smug and even superficially happy again, because lockdown meant a delay to everything, uncertainty, and more importantly the preservation of his comfortable home life. I spent my days managing the kids' remote schooling, keeping them sane and happy as their realities were turned upside down, and finding new ways to learn and develop myself in the absence of work. I dove headfirst into a number of different communities to start unpacking the person I was and to continue reconfiguring the woman I wanted to be. It was during this time that I clearly heard my calling towards stepping into my role as a shaman. I remember treading lightly with referring to myself as a "shaman" publicly. I didn't want anyone to think I was some new age crazy person just wantonly throwing around a role that holds ancestral and cultural significance for so many. A shaman, by definition, is a medicine woman or man who helps others to acknowledge and heal themselves through a variety of divination and spiritual and healing modalities. They are a person who stands in the gap of the physical, upper, and lower realms of reality reflecting not only the light but the so-called dark. I did a lot of healing work personally during the lockdown, and when we came out of lockdown, I performed a lot of healing work for people. This idea of me being a shaman was solidified not only through what I did to heal, but the darkness I had to experience to understand the value of healing.

That darkness fell at the end of April 2020 when I woke up with a discussion I had with my dad on my mind. The week before this particular day, my dad had mentioned that he had a brief yet odd conversation with Venom on Facebook. My dad saw "J. Pain," so he reached out via messenger, thinking it was me returning to Facebook. Instead, he found out that it was Venom and that he was going under "Junior Pain" there. "Junior" was a family nickname he never used to my knowledge. He also shared my disdain for Facebook when we would discuss it through the years, so it was peculiar to hear that he had a profile there. I thought it was an interesting finding when my dad brought it to my attention, but I mostly brushed it off. This day, in April of 2020, it came back up for me. I felt there was something more to know about him, so I decided to do a quick online search. In searching him online, I noticed he had way more addresses attributed to his record than I did. This was odd because we moved out at the same time and that meant our addresses from at least 2005 should have matched.

They didn't. As I scoured his online record more, I found a woman with his last name that wasn't his mother, sisters, or me. Naturally, I was thinking to myself, who is this woman running around with his last name other than myself? That was when I chose to pay $9.99 so I could see his full record and get more information on this woman. It turned out that this woman was not only using his last name, but she lived at the address of our first apartment together in 2005. What are the chances that someone who is using his last name would be living at an address he and I shared? The next piece of connective tissue came when I realized he kept that address tied to him until January of 2019. Why would he do that if this wasn't someone I should be interested in uncovering?

The first person I called was my brother. I gave him the whole scenario about this other woman who was gallivanting around town with his last name. He said to me, "I do work in that area quite often; I can always get a visual and pop by when I'm out there one day." We agreed this was a good course of action. This discussion between my brother and I was had on a Friday. When he returned to work the following Monday, he texted and snapchatted me that he was in Bayport near my old complex for work. I was floored. He said, "I'm about to roll up to the apartment now and see what's up." Essentially, he knocked on the door and acted as if he was lost in the complex. It took a while for the woman to answer. He said she seemed scared, but eventually she opened the door. They had a short discussion, but he described her as fair-skinned with freckles and noticed two kids playing in the living room. He couldn't get a good look at them.

My brother, as you can imagine, was not at all pleased with this preliminary finding. He was perhaps up close and personal with a woman Venom was involved with, and it infuriated him. He asked me what I wanted to do. I told him we must be patient and tread lightly. Walking up to someone's door had become somewhat of a social faux pas in light of the virus and so we couldn't go back there again. We had to use what we had to uncover the truth, and both of us were equally dedicated to this endeavor. I sat with what I knew for a few more days. All the while, this fool was coming home and sharing stories about his friend being suggestive towards a woman at his job. You really have to wonder how much arrogance and apathy one needs to have to come home to their estranged wife to chat about the infidelity going on in their friend circle during his own divorce. I can emphatically confirm he was not mentally well at this time.

On the Thursday night following our sting operation, I was up late chatting with my girlfriend, Celinda. I ran her down the gory details and that this woman had no digital footprint that I could find other than the address. She wanted to see for herself, so she ran her name as well, coming up with the same result of nothing. It was in that moment that she said something pivotal that would unlock the missing pieces. She asked me if I had ever gone through his stuff? My answer was "no." She said, "well bitch, you gonna go through his shit tonight." What I still laugh about until this day is how I thought I was on CSI with my kitchen gloves on, carefully tiptoeing up the stairs from my room to our living room to retrieve his bag. I had concerns about being caught; I mean he's a detective after all. I gently walked with his work bag in hand back to my room and started to investigate. The first thing I found was generic Cialis and Viagra. Apparently, my man was putting in work with assistance. The way I held back my cackling was superhuman. As I continued to rummage through the bag, I found an orange and a wad of receipts. In examining the receipts, there were quite a few from 2010 from a bank I wasn't aware he banked with that he was wiring various increments of money to someone named "LaTonya Johnson." I looked through more receipts and found one from the fall of 2019 for $1,100 dollars, again wired to a LaTonya Johnson. I sat with the name for a bit as it rang a bell. I remembered in 2009 coming home to a Western Union receipt for $400 that was addressed to LaTonya Johnson. I remember being furious because it was bill time, and I had no idea who this was. When I asked him who he had just given $400 to and who LaTonya Johnson was, he said she was a cousin that was going through a rough patch. I had asked him to never give out money again unless we discussed it. He apologized and agreed. Imagine my surprise to have this 2009 scenario come flooding back to inform me that it is very likely LaTonya Johnson was not a cousin, as he said, but a mistress. Judging by the extremely precise increments of money, it was even more apparent that this woman was receiving child support payments from him. All of these findings gave me enough ammunition to go to the culprit and get an admission.

That next day, I waited for him to come home, shower, and get settled. I quietly and calmly walked up to the bedroom and asked the kids to give us some privacy. I sat down on this teal floral print ottoman I had back then, and he said, "what's up!" I wanted to slap the taste out of his mouth at that point, but I continued diplomatically that he and I needed to have a discussion and that our relationship or what was left of it has been irreparably changed regardless of what he says. He responded dryly, "okay." I asked him if he knew a woman by the name of "Giselbertha." He said he didn't know her. I said it's interesting that you say you don't know her because she is walking around town with your last name and lives at our old address in Bayport. He went on to say that he didn't know who that was and that he would have to go there and see who that is. Let's just stop here for a moment. Why would you need to go see someone you claim you don't know? As my grandmothers used to say, "he thought I was a damn ass!" My blood was reaching a temperature that was starting to scare me, so I directed us to move on from that.

I went on to ask him clearly and frankly if he had fathered a child outside of our marriage. Venom, in all of his glory responded, "why would you ask me that?" I said, "it's a simple question with simple answers. Have you fathered a child outside of our marriage?" He looked down, grabbing his head, and took a deep sigh before he said, "maybe." He was playing games by answering me vaguely and all I was thinking was I should leap over this bed for him, but instead I played along. I probed further by asking, "if in the infinite possibility of multiverses, you had fathered a child, who would this child have been made with?" He answered, "with a young lady." In an unsettlingly soft way, I asked him if this "young lady" has a name? He hesitated, but then had the audacity to say, "well, you seem to know who it is, so why don't you just say it?" My anger is uncontrollable now and I say in a forthright manner, "these are not the games we're playing tonight, motherfucker. I know very well who it is, but I want you to tell me who this person is." Frustrated with the realization that he just got caught in this massive, reality-bending lie, he said, "her name is 'LaTonya Johnson'." To which I responded, "bingo, motherfucker!" The conversation continued, and I learned that this child was fathered while we were still dating in 2005, which means our oldest daughter was not his eldest child. It also meant that he went and asked my father for my hand in marriage and sat through every aspect of our wedding along with our best man, knowing that he had fathered a child.

Every pre-foreclosure or deficit in money was due to this secret he kept. His high blood pressure that I was always working so hard to research and cure over the years to no avail was the result of this dark secret that was eating away at him from the inside out. I will save the gory details of the realizations and happenings that occurred in the following weeks, apart from one incident. I had substantially revised our divorce stipulation after the unveiling of this outside child. One day in May of that year, I had to email him a few things. When he responded back, I noticed he had changed his real name to "Venom Pain." I thought at the time it was dark, but it is also spot on. When you think about how venom is often a vehicle for a slow and painful death, that is in effect what he was doing to me and to himself. The same pain that was imposed on him as a child was now what he served up in generous portions to whomever he was with. Love is a strange thing to someone who only knows pain. Relationships are a dangerous place for men and women who haven't begun to acknowledge and heal their pain.

A dangerous mind, in my opinion, is one that hasn't been explored or mastered. I learned in time that Venom was quite like Venom from the comics. He needed a host to carry on purposefully. For 17 years, I was a trusty host complete with a formidable vocabulary, unconditional love, ambition, and a desire to put better into the world. He used all of it to build some semblance of relevance for himself, but the darkness kept tugging at him. He couldn't hold my frequency or any superficially developed frequency without me or my family to siphon from. Without all of it, he is quite an empty vessel. I have often wondered if I was better off without him, but to wish him away is to recognize that my kids are who they are in part because of him as well. They are my greatest gift and, on that premise alone, I have to give thanks for the lessons even though they were tough.

> ***Rebel Elegance Reflection:*** *I was really stuck on whether this chapter should have a "rebel elegance" reflection or an "evolving soul" reflection. I went with rebel elegance because there are women who stay in abusive, soul-sucking, and toxic relationships for reasons stemming from lack of finances up to and including to keep up appearances. My marriage was abusive, and Venom was emotionally and mentally abusive. I still don't know the depths to what he is capable of, and I'm not sure I cared much upon uncovering everything. It takes a certain level of rebelliousness, this attitude*

that I won't do you as you did me, but my next chapter will speak volumes for my tenacity and resilience. When you can walk away with your kids in tow and several proverbial swords in your back, leaving behind the neighborhood, the schools, the mutual friends, and all the things that make a marriage societally relevant for the unknown; that shit is badass. Divesting yourself of an abusive relationship often needs to happen in phases for your safety and sometimes for your sanity. For wherever you find yourself on the continuum of breaking free, I salute you from the other side. It gets better and I am waiting for you along with your new life.

What did you learn from my story? If you are currently in an abusive or toxic relationship, write yourself a love letter. What do you need to hear today to keep going? What are you most excited about as you fight for the freedom to experience your new chapter in life?

Use the space below to document your rebel elegance reflections.

"BOUNDARIES"

December 28th, 2018

Don't penetrate me and never touch my soul.

Don't lust for me and never touch my heart.

Didn't you know diving deep into this sea of love with me is the best part?

Don't reach for my hand if you never tried to understand me.

Don't ask me to be your light, if you're unwilling to fight. My love is rare.

To be met with anything less would be impure and unfair.

I want to love and be loved without a care in the world.

Unrealistic?

I prefer to be optimistic.

There are layers to my existence. Getting to the treasure I have to offer isn't a chore, but a blessing for the right man. Love me deeply or leave me alone.

I AM
SPIRITUALLY
NOURISHED
BY
EVERYTHING
THAT
WAS
DESIGNED
TO DESTROY ME
AND ALL THINGS SENT TO ENLIGHTEN ME.

"THE GIFT OF EQUANIMITY"

January 29th, 2020

Everyone we meet is designed to teach us in this life. Based on our own understanding, we give each lesson a grade of good or bad, pleasant or unpleasant, necessary or unnecessary, important or fruitless. The key is not to rush or fake your processing of the people or situations involved in your life's journey, but rather to ensure you are able to receive the lessons within the lesson without it triggering you or provoking some other emotional response. This is the pinnacle of approaching our finite lives on Earth with equanimity.

What a bag of tricks we've been sold about what this life is all about. So much of our suffering stems from our own qualitative assessment of how things are going in life hour-to-hour, month-to-month, year-to-year, and so on.

With maturity and inner wisdom, we come to understand that experiences are just experiences and that it is our human expectations, conditioning, and fears that cause us to perceive a situation as desirable or undesirable. The observer of life has a much different vantage point on the state of affairs. The observer sees situations, whether past or present, as opportunities for perspective and growth. We may enjoy some experiences more than others, but if perspective and growth have happened, we have succeeded in those exercises.

There are an infinite number of souls we meet in a lifetime, yet we get hung up on one singular expression of humanity in love, friendships, etc. The ultimate goal of equanimity is not to turn a blind eye to our emotions or to dismiss the reality that you will experience roadblocks that will rock everything you thought you knew about humanity. This is to suggest that you can let go of feeling overwhelmed by every little thing that happens to you. You can surrender to better experiences. You can be at home with the mundane aspects of life. Life expands and contracts based on how you choose to see it and participate in it. Equanimity is about taking incremental steps towards creating different narratives about what is happening in your life. Start now. Start small. See things from a higher perspective.

> ***Evolving Soul Reflection:*** *Achieving balance in life requires us to look at things from a higher perspective. Life is a series of events that are never satisfying enough until you are on the other side of those experiences or marching closer to the end of life. Equanimity invites us to savor everything that occurs throughout our life...every bit of it.*
>
> *How can you be more present with both the pleasant and unpleasant aspects of your life? Where did the notions of "good" and "bad" begin in your story? How has that colored how you see your life? How can you identify the roots of your frustration so you can see the purpose in this experience you are having?*

Use the space below to document your evolving soul reflections. I'm glad you're alive. You should be too.

"There is beauty in everything we do. We must change our perception about our hardships."

~ Gail Whitlow "Kanienkehaka" (Mohawk)

"THE JOKE OF WOKE"

June 5th, 2019

It's simply not enough to just be "woke". I know this may sting some who feel they have reached some sort of zenith in their existence because their eyes have been opened to the commotions and devotions of life. Here's what I would like to know. Why be "woke" when the goal is to be aware and connected? Don't diminish your power to the banality of a buzzword. The possession of knowledge and lucidity of your consciousness alone does not qualify you in the school of life. It's about the actions you take once you have been enlightened...awakened to the illusions that envelope us individually and societally. Free yourself from labels, shed the necessary layers, meet your darkness with love and compassion, and heal so you can rise in service.

"THE EXPRESSION OF POSSIBILITY"

April 1st, 2019

The old school term of "Don't hate, participate" couldn't have been truer. So long as you are here and breathing, everything is possible, and nothing is impossible. We often scoff at others with audacious goals, otherworldly experiences, and larger-than-life aspirations, but they are the true magicians, alkhemists among us. They exploit the possibility to test what they have the ability to accomplish. Sometimes the magic trick works and sometimes it doesn't. The point is the power of their belief in what is possible is often more potent, and it allows them to live outside of the parameters of the mundane.

As I allude to many times over in this book, life is a timed experiment. You can spend your time setting up the experiment, theorizing about the plan, or you can get right to the heart of the matter and start testing several hypotheses over time so you can come back to the lab with new and better answers that are worthy of further exploration and eventually execution.

We know a likkle something about why we're here and how the laws of the universe work. It is at the very point that you have been granted some wisdom to go on that you realize you have only scratched the surface.

Look at the places in your life where you have yet to expand your perspective, reasoning, and consciousness. Allow yourself to seek answers beyond what logic tells you. Spring has sprung and so should your mind. Give birth to something new within you.

Use the space below to document your purposeful soul reflections. Write down three ways you will start to explore what is possible in your own life.

“THE TRUTH OF LIFE”

June 15th, 2018

Life is not linear nor is it predictable. We are urged to achieve and plan as if those older than us don’t already know that 60% or more of life’s events are out of our hands. I wish more people told me my happiness was gold and not to be sold. I wish more people told me that feeling and doing things from my heart was the best part. I wish I knew sadness and darkness was inevitable. I would have learned earlier to appreciate those feelings more. No one warned me that thoughts matter, because what we think, we create. I thank the heavens that darkness fell, and my inner work began before it was too late. I’m in my mid-thirties learning how to feel more than I think. Somebody before me knew better. I just know it. The trouble is they were too filled with pride to show it. Life isn’t linear. What a surprise! Its beauty and wonder often brings tears to my eyes. To learn is a blessing, even by fire. Taking this little life of mine by the balls and squeezing it until there is nothing more is my deepest desire.

In Buddhism, it is believed that desire and ignorance are at the root of all human suffering. I spent my young adult years craving more money, more prestige, more material things. While they all brought me a semblance of happiness and achievement, there was a certain emptiness to my constant mindset of always having to do more and get more. I learned in recent years that my need to always be acquiring the next accolade came from a place of lack. That mentality didn't spring up serendipitously; I discovered it is another generational gem and cue I acquired along the way. I grew up watching my mother work two and three jobs at times. We weren't poor and we weren't rich. My parents' inability to co-create and manifest better came from a lack of connection they had to themselves and each other. Money came and it went, as it will often disappear where we lack gratitude for what is. I don't think Buddhism means for us to be poor and not have things, but I believe it is urging us to understand that nothing in this world is ours. Every person we meet, every dollar we make, every luxury we enjoy is on loan to us as a blessing in this quantum moment known as our life. To become attached to worldly possessions is to suffer because what becomes of you when they are no longer there? How will you qualify yourself beyond the titles, possessions, and accomplishments? When I started to consider all these factors, I started to practice detachment and gratitude much more. It's not to say that I don't enjoy the fruits of my labor; in fact, I feel I enjoy them more now as I am more detached. It is the knowing that they are all blessings on loan to me that allows me to let go when I have had my fill and relish in them with my presence for the time I am granted.

I will follow my desires to the ends of the earth, because it is what my heart wants the most. I desire without craving or addiction. After suffering due to my attachment to what I have thought my life should be, I have resigned to a more delicious path of following my heart without expectation of a particular outcome. It is the serendipity and magic of life that gets lost in the planning, doing, and acquiring. Figuring out what I desire, acknowledging it, and giving it to the universe to sort out in my favor has been my rebellious path of least resistance.

Time to do some reflecting, rebels. *What have you identified as some of your more challenging behaviors and attributes? How have these aspects helped or harmed you throughout life? Part of becoming better versions of yourself is being able to give yourself grace and kindness. How can you begin to acknowledge and love those aspects of yourself more?*

Use the space below to document your rebel elegance reflections.

WHAT I WISH MORE PEOPLE KNEW

I interviewed with an organization called "The Inheritance Project" during our first shelter-in-place. I first attended their workshop out of curiosity and in honor of my "7" spiritual sabbatical/loner year. I just knew there was some generational coding that needed unearthing, and it was there that I found more fractals of myself I didn't know needed acknowledgement. I was also going through somewhat of an identity crisis where I was slowly liberating myself from the hell of carrying my assumed married last name which was now stained by "Venom Pain" in epic ways, and my desire to go back in time and be who I once was, which was "Janine Nicole Dennis." It's one thing to be tethered to the family given to you in divine fashion from birth. It is quite another to be tied in name to someone whose actions and behaviors have caused hurt, pain, and damage without your consent and without a care. The Inheritance Project will go down as an experience that reminded me of my sovereignty.

One of the questions in the interview was, "What do you wish other people knew about you, your inheritance, and identity?" My heart started to hurt immediately, as if there was something there I had been choking back for far too long. I shared with them the following:

"I wish people knew that my perceived and observed strength has been hard won. I have had to navigate at least a generation of anger and dysfunction to get to where I am today. None of my achievements landed in my lap. I had to work hard and very much to my own deficit at times. I have had a complex for a long time about letting my light shine but so brightly, because of being chastised within my family for being smart, wise, ahead-of-my-time ambitious, truthful, etc. In short, life hasn't been a cakewalk; there has been a lot to unlearn and unpack. So, if my identity and persona show a well-adjusted person it's because I've done the work. That aside, my inheritance, my story isn't only about difficulty and trauma. I come from good stock. My family is comprised of hardworking (almost to a fault), educated, and superbly intelligent humans. We are healers, caring people who are a mixed bag of creatives, builders, healthcare workers, innovators, and civil service professionals. We're upstanding citizens, and yet there is a primal rage within us all that can be ignited at a moment's notice."

It is easy to laud and praise people whose lived experiences look grand from afar but whose fine print is blurred to you. Never wish for anyone's life but your own. Jealousy is an emotionally lazy and dangerous characteristic when it goes unacknowledged or unchecked. There is nothing anyone can have that you can't. Honor your own moments no matter how painful and grueling they may be. Your journey was designed with you in mind. What you covet in others you have no real proximity to. It's all romantic and sexy when people you know or are familiar with appear to lead lives that result in societally attractive outcomes. Ask people what they had to sacrifice. Ask more people about the pain they endured to become whole. Ask more "successful" people about their life's terms and conditions and how they chose to navigate them. That's where the real glory and story begins.

> ***Evolving Soul Reflection:*** *My Grandma Marie would often say in her Trini Patois: "Doh watch people." Essentially, she meant don't watch what people are doing and focus on yourself. She would often tell me the more you watch, the less you see. In other words, you are never given full command of what is going on in another person's life because it is either meant to teach a lesson or present as a reflection. This life is a game of you vs. you. When you start playing it that way, you will decrease and eradicate a lot of your self-worth issues.*
>
> *What is your life's fine print? How are you navigating the "terms and conditions" of your journey? What can you do today to focus more on what you are designed to do here?*

Use the space below to document your evolving soul reflections.

THERE IS
SOMETHING
INTRIGUING
ABOUT
SOMEONE
WHO WALKS
CONFIDENTLY
WITH THEIR
SHADOWS
HAND-IN-HAND.

"SUBMITTING TO ME"

February 10th, 2019

Timing is everything when it comes to the stuff of life. People come into your life serendipitously and exit without a trace. As sentient beings we think we know best and even more laughable, we think we have control over the cadence of the events in our lives. Never say what you won't do, because life will always find ways to make you eat those words. A year ago, I couldn't stomach the things I have done and am prepared to do now. More than a year after a whirlwind of a love connection, I am excited to start a new chapter and to be more exploratory than I have ever been in my life. BDSM was wildly new when it was introduced to me by "Dr. Medley." I was not willing to be dominated, and he has not proven he is worthy of me submitting myself to him. I can see that, when done right with someone you love and trust, there can be a deeper level of intimacy between you and your partner. So, what was the point of our experience with one another? The point is this time in my life is calling me to expand with life. I am willing to try, experiment, and surrender. The lessons are deeper than the obvious. This is a lot coming from me. It appears this is a time for me to be free and do exactly what I want. Honoring my pleasure is my divine right. I get it now. I need to submit to myself. It was never about a sexual act or a man. "Dr. Medley" came to teach me where I had lost my passion and zeal for Janine. As much as I would love to prioritize what everyone else needs and wants from me, my life cannot be on hold any longer. I have given to everyone selflessly, but it is time I put Janine first for once. There is something sexy and titillating about that notion.

> ***Rebel Elegance Reflection:*** *Sexuality is about more than sex; it is about pleasure and allowing yourself to surrender to the deliciousness of life. Time is more than a construct. It is the synchronistic beauty by which things unfold to create meaning in our lives. We have to release shame and judgment of ourselves and others if we are to live our lives to the fullest. Pleasure is your divine right, whether that be a passionate night with someone you connect with between the sheets or enjoying your favorite ice cream. Be rebellious in your pursuit of it.*
>
> *What has life shown you about the divine timing in your own life? What were you taught about how to receive pleasure? What can you do today to invite more pleasure into your daily experiences?*

Use the space below to document your rebel elegance reflections.

“SEX AS A DIVINATION TOOL”

April 23rd, 2021

“I feel like this year will be what 2019 was for you. Something is opening up... Not just my legs, but that too.” ~ One of the soul sistas

In a sea of the many conversations I have with my circle of trust, sex and its divine purpose come up often. One of my dear friends had shared with me that she was called to see sexual experiences as a divine connector to enlightenment. My response was the following:

“The act of sex is indeed a divination tool. All powerful creatrixes and alkhemists have mastered the art of purposeful merging with another. That experience of the highest level of pleasure leads to other blessings and more joy if done right. I got cracked open in 2018 and I ain’t never been the same since. I think part of our journey this go-around is to be more sexually explorative. We come from a culture that doesn’t exactly exalt ‘the act’ except through sexual innuendo or the exploitation of women’s sensuality and sexuality in the media and music. Growing up, there wasn’t a whole lot of empowerment for our own desires and wants, let alone a masterclass on setting healthy boundaries in our sexual life."

The most revolutionary discussion I had as a child was this one time my mom spoke of masturbation in front of my Guyanese Grandmother. Who told her to do this? My grandmother was mortified and went into a whole tirade in her patois. She said, and I quote, "what manner of foolishness is this? Allyuh keep on, deh Lard (Lord) is vex with us." It was a funny conversation but also confusing as I had respect for both perspectives. Was my pleasure an affront to God, or was it divine and steeped in God's approval? I barely had a solid concept of what God was and here I was considering if it or he would approve of me masturbating. I had no answers and I damn sure wasn't brave enough to ask more questions, nor was I willing to admit that I was already a pro at it and loving the way it made me feel.

Up until about 2017, there were still so many sexual desires and wants that lay dormant for me. Many things seemed taboo, and there was a source of shame for me around things I wanted to experience. Between 2018 and 2020, I unraveled all the shame, stories, and blocks I was creating to my pleasure. My liberation and journey towards learning what I liked as a grown woman was eye-opening. I achieved it through celibacy (believe it or not) and intentional and careful exploration of everything from BDSM to attending soft play parties to learn more about Tantra Sex. I traveled well beyond the confines of my comfort to unearth a healthier and more expansive version of myself. This is a version of me that places exponential value on my pleasure and is now more comfortable than ever, being both sensual and sexual as it suits me. I understand that I have a responsibility to wield that power carefully. I also understand that it is not my responsibility to hide that part of me out of fear of how it will be perceived, or the ways people may choose to engage with my energy due to their own lack of composure, respect, and mastery of self.

How did I do this specifically?

I did what I do in business. I strategically placed myself in environments that would force me to experience something new. I'm not a fan of porn per se, but I bought myself tickets to Exxxotica, a porn convention in the fall of 2019. It was not nearly as taboo as I expected. Sure, there were vendors at every turn looking for you to spend your dollars on sex toys and virtual experiences. A new toy never hurt anyone, and I hadn't bought one since the early 2000s. It was time. The young lady I encountered at one of the many boutiques onsite was extremely pleasant and quickly brought me up to speed on the latest and greatest sex toys. That was a win.

That night, I spent most of my time being tantalized by the goings on, not so much as a participant but as a lover of life and perhaps a voyeur. Next, I attended a few breakout sessions on various sex sub-topics. One notable one was the one with Jet Setting Jasmine and King Noire, on the art of BDSM. They are both well-known Black, Ethical Sex Educators and Porn Stars. Next, I made my way to King Heff's area of the convention center and where I ended up having a conversation and lesson in submission I didn't know I needed that day. My last stop was with a tarot reader who also gave a great breakout class on "divine feminine" energy and how to use it. I don't typically gravitate to tarot readers because I am a tarot reader myself, but I felt guided. When I got to her, we greeted one another, and she started to shuffle her cards. Every card was a sign of the abundance I already felt in the pit of my stomach. Her earring had fallen off, which caused her to ask me if I was aware of orishas and if I had devoted myself to any. I told her yes, Yemaya and Oshun. She said she knew something was up when her earring dropped off. She pulled out some cowrie shells and other things she hadn't for others before me. She told me I needed to prepare rituals for my orishas. She went on to explain that the upper realms, my ancestors and guides, were trying to figure out how they wanted to use me. In that tarot reading, I learned what I needed to do to call in both my healing and blessings. I saw at one point she was hesitant to tell me more and I asked her if she saw me becoming pregnant again. She said, "yes, they are preparing your body to bring forth another child." My mind was aptly blown. I thanked her for all the things she told me and left the convention full and grateful thereafter. My night ended in a deeply contemplative ride back to NY, smoking a CBD pre-roll whilst enjoying a NSFC (Not Safe for Children) playlist, and followed by me stopping at my favorite diner for some pancakes and eggs before heading home.

I can already hear the gasps in advance for what you just read, but that should signal you to do some more work on yourself to explore why the topic of sex and any of its sub-topics creates that response from you. By most people's estimation, I became a mom and wife to have a slow and quiet death ravage "Janine Nicole" for the sake of all things politically correct and proper. Motherhood and wifedom are not where you and your sexuality or individuality go to die. Yes, I still love sex. Yes, I smoke weed and enjoy my share of edibles. I've even had my share of psychedelic journeys to heal. And so what? It took me a lot of years to catch on, but I realized it was fair and equitable for me to still explore, to be curious, to be fully "Janine Nicole," and never lose her again. I'm raising two daughters currently and soon to be raising another two princesses. I can't have them going out into the world not understanding the full capability of their human bodies. I refuse for them to be bereft of understanding the importance of sexual health and the spiritual implications of lying with another. I'll be damned if they go through life feeling ashamed and unable to fully express and experience their sexuality and sensuality. They will grow up with healthy examples and narratives surrounding motherhood and constructs of commitment should they decide they want to be married or in a committed relationship with someone down the line. These experiences showed me how little women's pleasure is centered in our society. It's even worse for BIPOC women. Where do we turn for positive examples of sexuality and sensuality? Like it or not, that is where sex educators like Jet Setting Jasmine, King Noire, and King Heff come in. You don't have to watch porn or be steeped in sexual taboos to respect a lifestyle or even to learn from it. I couldn't do what they do, but I'm immensely grateful for what it has awakened within me as I sought to reinvent myself.

It's a new day.

I'm grateful that I allowed myself a few years to be curious and explore. I'm equally grateful that after all of my bacchanalin was over I allowed my body to rest in the comfort of celibacy and the conscious choice of monogamy. It was a powerful reset for me and has elevated my intimacy and relationship with my current lover to otherworldly proportions.

> ***Rebel Elegance Reflection:*** *I didn't give you all the tea on purpose. We must keep some of those juicier moments for our rocking chairs in our golden years, or maybe for the next book. People are not monolithic. We have many different sides to our personas, each deserving of full expression. It is incredibly strange that the topic of sex is so taboo in a country that glorifies the objectification of women and exploits sex not just on our shores, but globally via a global sex trafficking network. You can't just shield kids from sex one day, then in the next few years have "the talk" only to never fill in the gaps, which later in their lives leads to you asking them for grandkids once they are adults. Find positive ways to have healthy discussions about sex not only as a family, but with yourself. The quality of your sex life is equal to how confident, secure, safe, and free you feel to express your wants and needs.*
>
> *Relax your genitals! Do some kegels if you know what's up. Not even I get to see what you will write*

here. Here's where you get to be as raw and vulnerable as you would like to. I encourage you to dive in. What emotions come up for you as you consider your sex life currently? What are some of the stories that inform your approach to sexuality? How can you invite more curiosity and exploration into your sexual and sensual life?

Use the space below to document your rebel elegance reflections.

"ATTACHMENT IS THE ROOT OF ALL EVIL"

September 14th, 2019

Attachment is the source of suffering. Everything is impermanent. Feelings, emotions, circumstances, and people will always come and go. When we realize that everything we see is just a representation of various lessons we are meant to learn, we can detach more and more, resulting in more inner peace and less turmoil.

That failed relationship, that interview that didn't result in you getting the job, that one thought that led you down a rabbit hole of negative self-talk are just manifestations of how your inner world dances with the external. The more we can detach and flow, the more we will enjoy and hopefully be able to observe this experience we call life for what it is. No thing or person is permanent, which is why it is so necessary to not only enjoy the moments, but to be fully secure and grounded in yourself above all else.

THERE'S
FREEDOM
IN
UNCONDITIONAL
LOVE.
I NO LONGER
HAVE TO BE
SOMETHING
I'M NOT.

DEFINING REBEL ELEGANCE

September 15th, 2019

This was the day I spoke aloud and said the following:

"My next chapter will not be like the rest. We all want authenticity until we have to witness it in all its audacious, non-linear, messy glory."

A new chapter had long been en queue for me. For as great of a writer, go-getter, and alkhemist as I am, I couldn't have written this story I'm living. It's fun, interesting, difficult at times, mind-blowing, and messy enough to trigger my recovering perfectionist ways.

All the same, it has molded me into a different character with an unconventional story. A story that conventional people close their minds, ears, and hearts to. It's all good, because one of the benefits of my journey has been an ever-decreasing supply of fucks to give for the critique or opinions of others.

We say to one another "do you boo," but that more often than not means, "do you" so I can understand or "in accordance with what is palatable for me." I encourage you all to say less about what others do and focus on what you do. I urge you to do more cheering and less fearing of those of us who bravely and sometimes ignorantly color outside of the proverbial lines. We, the rebels, outcasts, and weirdos are the subjects of poetry, best-selling novels, blockbuster movies, famous paintings, and the saucy stories you love to read in the tabloids accompanied by your morning tea or coffee.

What does it mean to exhibit "rebel elegance"?

Rebel elegance is the act of purposefully standing in both defiance and opposition of any expression of yourself that is conventional, safe, orderly, or socially acceptable with eloquence, fortitude, and grace. Difference is an affront to order. It is seen as chaotic and an anomaly to normalcy. To the degree that we are all over "normal," "new normals," and anything that doesn't allow space for us all to be fully operating in our humanity, I say we obliterate our archaic ways of thinking and move forward with rebel elegance in tow.

> ***Rebel Elegance Reflection:*** *In May of 2019, Inc.com Writer Heather R. Morgan penned an article called, "Why Being Perfect Will Actually Screw You Over." In the article, she warns against diminishing marginal returns and the relativity of perfection. People who have a healthy relationship with failure and approach to life in general have more fun from what I have observed. They have already spotted the inherent imperfection in the do-gooders of the world and decided that those narratives never need to inform who they are or what they are becoming. Humans are wild and primal by nature. While I'm certain we have benefited greatly by creating some order throughout millennia, we are dangerously marching towards so much order that it's stifling people. When people feel repressed or subjugated to a certain set of norms, no shocker here, they rebel. I am merely here to give people the middle ground perspective in the midst of revolution and on the heels*

of full-on rebellion.

So, here's the question:

How can you begin to embrace those "unconventional" aspects of yourself? What would it mean to you to fully express yourself if you knew you would be accepted?

Use the space below to document your rebel elegance reflections.

PRISMATIC THINKING

Prism: noun. "a transparent body that is bounded in part by two nonparallel plane faces and is used to refract or disperse a beam of light or 'a medium that distorts, slants, or colors whatever is viewed through it'."

I believe my life has been the culmination of me consciously and unconsciously skipping through timelines and passing through many wormholes and portals at the divine right time. As you have read, so much has happened in my 39 years on this rotating rock and yet there is a part of me that feels like the clock reset itself somewhere along the way; so in effect, my life has just begun. In the early 2010s, I remember having this vision that this timekeeper, watcher-of-sorts started lovingly but earnestly rewriting the plan for my life from page 1; not as if nothing had happened before that moment, but to suggest that a significant cycle of burdens and lessons was finally over because I was now intentionally co-creating my life in accordance with the divine plan again. Should this vision trip you up a bit, I highly suggest watching the movie "The Adjustment Bureau." It was suggested to me by Dr. Medley some years ago. Admittedly, it made me cry at the time as it is a bit of an otherworldly love story that reminded me of us, but more importantly, it codifies my theories and understanding of why things unfold as they do in this prismatic way.

I have always loved rainbows and anything that can reflect light. Rainbows not only make me happy, but they became daily beacons of hope at times where things were being rearranged in my life for my good. Those who have followed me on social media for some time had a front-row seat for the documentation of each of them. Literally, since elementary school, the knowledge that light and certain colors traveled at different speeds was always an interesting phenomenon to me. According to the University of Wisconsin-Madison's "The Wonders of Physics" website, "A prism works because the different colors of light travel at different speeds inside the glass. Because the colors of light travel at different speeds, they get bent by different amounts and come out all spread out instead of mixed up."

In so many ways, aren't all humans two sides of the same energy bound by a single source, yet living and breathing distortions of consciousness? None of us are one way all of the time. As I have illustrated throughout this book, we are predisposed to conditioning from a familial, societal, and cultural standpoint. The building blocks of what we inevitably become start at birth and have far-reaching implications that express themselves well beyond what our genetics and time in womb gestating would dictate. All of these conditions will have us all seeing each other and everything we encounter on Earth through a single lens if we allow it.

What prismatic thinking offers us is this ability to see everything as they are through the prism of life. If you choose to see life as linear and monochromatic, it will give you just that. It doesn't discontinue bending in technicolor, but your lens will never cheat you from your own limited perspective. At its core, prismatic thinking is the ability to see a single human or occurrence from multiple sides, giving each their right to their respective expressions. There is no good or bad in the prism, just different speeds of light, necessary distortions, and a lot of spectrum. When you practice prismatic thinking, it becomes easier for you to place everything and everyone in their rightful place along the continuum of life. The first sign that you are being called to "prismatic thinking" will be inherent in your ability to recognize that many things can be true at once. We often waste a lot of time and energy wondering why things don't operate in the way we think they should. Prismatic thinking empowers you to be more of an observer of things than judge and jury. In your more enlightened moments, you will not only be able to recognize the variety of thought and disposition in others, but you will come to appreciate that everyone is traveling at a unique and purposeful frequency and speed of light. It is important to note that no one person is relegated to one color band along the Roy G. Biv spectrum for the duration of their life, but where and how we meet one another at any given time is indeed fixed. From this perspective, we have no choice but to be in acceptance of where each of us is in life, when we meet, and all of the cascading circumstances that stem from that premise.

Let's have a look at politics as an example of something that gets people out of sorts. In the U.S. specifically, there are two parties that predominantly drive politics, and those parties are the Republicans and Democrats. If you tune into what is said about each of the parties, the Democrats tend to be the freedom fighting party, marginalized groups party of choice, pro-science discovery, pro-government-spending. I'm paraphrasing here and yes, there is much more spectrum than what I am illustrating here in both parties; but this is the bulk of what I have heard of both of these parties in the 20 years I have become of age to vote. The Republicans on the other hand have been the face of bigotry, modern day slavery, anti-government spending unless it is to fund our national defense complex to wage conflicts and wars with countries we have a vested interest in economically or for resources. They have equally been known for being anti-immigrant, pro-life, and proponents of conflating the obvious issues within religion with politics in a country whose law of the land professes liberties and freedoms associated with both.

How is prismatic thinking helpful when examining the role of these political parties?

1. Acknowledging that economic power and self-interest are central reasons for why both parties operate as they do.
2. Being contemplative about the fact that both of these parties are complicit in creating the gradual and current separation and deterioration of our so-called union.
3. We do need to slow or at a minimum reallocate our government spending, but perhaps you got too caught up with the racial stench currently plaguing the Republicans to admit that this is true.
4. How many times will marginalized groups allow politicians into their communities and houses of worship to coerce your vote before they are forced to do what is in the best interest of these groups?
5. Might our elected officials be a mirror with which to see everything both promising and problematic in society? We have a hand in electing them, yet we spend so much energy fighting over ideologies instead of finding the common ground between ourselves.

I think we can all agree that politicians like so many other things are part of the prism of life with all its spectrum and distortions. Are the politicians inherently the problem or is it the flawed systems and structures they operate within? I'll stop here. I'm not here to convince you that these are for sure the right questions to be asking ourselves as it pertains to our political system, but hopefully you can see that by taking a peek into the prism to examine these questions, we would have much more to consider and discuss than what our one-sided snap judgements and opinions offer.

My hope for you all is that you see prismatic thinking as a relevant vehicle for having more expansive and heart-centered conversations. Moreover, I hope it helps people to not just think outside of the box, but to create a sri yantra (a sacred geometric shape) and think both within and outside of the parameters of that.

Evolving Soul Reflection: *The degradation of critical thinking and diplomacy in our modern society is both startling and disheartening. To know me is to know that I have pretty strong views across a plethora of topics, but the two things that are stronger than any view I hold are my zeal for curiosity and a healthy debate. In my work, I have had to train and teach people who I know hold extremely different views than my own and who perhaps wouldn't sacrifice their ideals even with the knowledge that those ideals could harm me or other humans. The truth is, I have managed diplomatic and even loving conversations with these types because of my ability to apply prismatic thinking to every interaction I have. This doesn't mean I am perfect. I'm not. It just means that more often than not I choose to listen and to challenge my own views, because I have discovered that ultimately it will make me a more formidable opponent even if they choose to remain closed off and self-interested.*

How would you describe the way you think currently? Do you find it difficult to see things from multiple vantage points? What can you do to start incorporating "prismatic thinking" into your everyday interactions?

Use the space below to document your evolving soul reflections.

"LOVE KNOWS NO BOUNDS"

February 19th, 2020

None of us knows the day or time when love will visit us. When it does, we are often unprepared and riddled with years of conditioning and fears that we question how we could be worthy to be in its presence. Love doesn't show up ethically, morally, or based on societal conventions. When it shows up, it does so authentically. It is the highs of all highs and the secret whisper of our hearts. Love doesn't care about relationship status, monogamy, or commitment. These are the things we attach to this universal essence to justify our need for order and attachment. Love is easy when we can allow it to just be. People and fear get in its way. Love does not harm or hurt. It is our wounded souls that make it so.

In this new decade, we, the people of Planet Earth may have to admit we don't know much about life, relationships, or love. We will have to admit wholeheartedly that much of what we learned about any of the above-mentioned things is outdated, if not obsolete.

There is a new consciousness afoot that doesn't conform to societal norms, external validation, or conventional education.

My awakening and cycles in life and love in recent years has taught me about the impermanence of things. I have learned that love may require me setting the one I love free many times over to walk their own path such that it doesn't infringe on my own. I have learned that love in its purest form is easy, but that it's the "human" in us all that often gets in the way. I have learned that love is the great equalizer and yet, so few are willing to sacrifice what keeps them stuck in misery for a chance to experience bliss. Love is as grand as it is tragic. What I pray we learn as a sentient species is that the rules of engagement in life are always shifting and changing. The universe isn't tethered to one perspective of itself, and we shouldn't be either. "The Absurdity of Doing You" is grounded in your ability to allow your life to twist, turn, pivot, bloom, contract, and be in all its glory. There will never be another story of "You." Let love in, even if your own love is all you have. Make your existence an iconic one.

> ***Rebel Elegance Reflection:*** *As you have read, my life has been a collective of events that fit together in the perfect puzzle. I have grown from the confines of darkness towards the light of possibility, expansion, and love. Hopefully, you can see that love was present all along. Love was present in my upbringing. Love was my liberation and the source of my rebellion. Love is my children, my work, my legacy. This life is absurd and grand, mundane and inconsequential. I hope that my shifts, pivots, evolutions, and revolutions help you see the grandeur of your own life.*
>
> *How will you use rebel elegance in your own life? What can you do today to liberate yourself a bit more? What aspect of your life needs more love? What are you willing to do to become a magnet for love in all aspects of your life?*

Hey, you glorious rebel YOU! Use the space below to document your last rebel elegance reflection. Keep being contemplative and curious about your journey. Be the powerful alkhemist I know you can be. I believe in you.

Xo,
Janine Nicole

DEDICATED WITH LOVE TO:

My grandparents: Kathleen Fraser, Mavis Marie Dennis, Carl E. Dennis, Jacob Wills, and Clarice Wills who all have transitioned. You are the greats and the few who truly saw me for who I was. Thank you for being a confidant to the confidant.

To my parents, Brenda and Anthony Dennis: who are too cool for school and whose lives and presence in my life continue to inspire me to greater heights of evolution. Thank you for being the earthly guides I needed. Daddy, you decided to leave this plane earlier than I ever expected, but thank you for your protection, laughter, and example. I know what to do. I love you!

To my Aunt Bev a.k.a. Auntie Boof: You have been like a guardian angel to me. Thank you for guiding me along this journey called life and being one of my biggest fans. Love you!

To my brother Tony, who lives by his own rules much to the dismay of everyone around him but has a heart of gold and intelligence far surpassing most. Thank you for standing for me always, and in all ways. You have been a huge support system for me. It's you and I in every lifetime. I love you beyond words!

To my prima/sister-cousin, Lauren, some of my greatest healing has been done over the course of our marathon phone calls or in your home. You are the most gracious and loving person I know. I wanted you to know in specific how your love, support, and divine reflection has positively impacted my life. I love you forever and a day. Thank you for loving me as you do.

To my babies, Eleni, Grace, Analiesa, Bryce, and Elyse: You five embody the best parts of humanity. You all are so smart, deeply intuitive, unique, funny, goofy, creative, and kind. You are little lights in our lives that we don't take for granted. My little starseeds on this plane shielding me in an unimaginable love. My heart is full. Thank you for making it so. You all make me want to be better and do better. I can't thank each of you enough for changing my life in the best way possible. We are a tribe of Black love, excellence, and greatness. Never forget that. I love you all!

To my forever love, Terrence: My king, you are my prayers answered in the flesh. My years of tears were nourishment and clearing for the extraordinary love I never saw coming. The world literally had to stop for our universes to collide. The bliss of the collision and ride with you is indescribable, yet delicious. You, Grace, and Elyse are the greatest surprise and gifts I could ever receive. You are my best friend, my lover, the Osiris to my Isis, my business partner, beloved patriarch of our growing blended tribe, and most importantly, my one true love. I love you forever and 13,000 more lifetimes.

To my soul family: There are far too many of you all to name, but as I like to say, what is understood never needs to be said. You all know who you are and what you mean to me. When I was going through one of the darkest yet illuminating seasons of my life, you all chipped in on my rebuild in some form or fashion. I stand here today as a renewed woman of purpose because of your love, candor, support, and prayers. My gratitude for you all knows no bounds. I love each of you immensely. There are a few people I have to shout out a few in specific who not only had a front-row seat to my evolution but helped to rebuild and restore me cell by cell.

Cashel Campbell thank you for being a confidant, a healer, and for shifting my pain in a way that became transformative. You are a true medicine woman and I adore you.

Joanne Wolf, thank you for illuminating the truth of who I am and giving me a roadmap for my destiny while playing out this character of "Janine Nicole." Your guidance has led me to a comprehensive knowledge of myself and the greatest loves of my life, one of them being me loving me.

Liliana, mi hermana, how did an impromptu drop into my

sister circle result in such a rich connection where we ended up helping each other understand the underpinnings and purpose in our existences? We have spent hours upon hours supporting one another. I am thankful for your medicine, your heart, and your light.

Dorothy, we were brought together when we needed one another the most. You gave me the gift of opportunity, healing through cannabis, and true sisterhood. A lifetime of friendship doesn't dictate the quality. Our short time knowing one another has brought so much love and light to my life. I am grateful for your kindness, your heart, and our soul connection.

Blue and Ravneet, we have never formally met, but no one can deny us the bond I share with each of you. You know where the newest of bones are hidden and you never once judged. Our souls grew up together from incessantly watching tarot readings to making sense of our individual awakenings to coming into greater realizations of self-love and acceptance. It's been a wild ride! Thank you for the sisterhood. I look forward to the day that I can hug you both separately.

Kim, what a blessed and unexpected gift you have been to me and the kids. There is no question we have been guides and comforting soulmates to one another in every lifetime. Thank you for seeing me and gently guiding me lovingly towards my current shameless and ascended existence. I love you like a plate of oxtails with extra gravy pon di rice. You are my sister-in-evolution eternally.

Anne, what a bright light you are. I knew you were magnificent even before we broke bread together in Philly. Your heart is so big and your care and love for me is enduring and so appreciated. Thank you for being the very best soul sista. My life is so much brighter and beautiful because you are in it.

Trish, you have a heart of gold. We were sent to one another at the divine right time in our respective evolutions.

The heavens knew I needed someone with not an ounce of judgment in their soul and with a life story that would inspire me to keep going despite the darkness looming at the time. We have cried, laughed, danced, and created memories that will last us well into our golden years. Thank you for loving me as you do. You are my ace and I love you so very much.

The "Namigas," Sarah, Keirsten, Tiffany, thank you for walking your respective journeys with me when none of us knew what the fuck we were doing or what was happening to us. If there is such a thing as hell, we have certainly been there and back together. Building professional relevancy amidst personal turmoil is not for the faint of heart, but you all have always kept me fed, lifted in prayer and cared for. Thank you from the bottom of my heart. I love you all.

To my spiritual team in the great beyond, spirit guides, White Tiger Totem, ancestors both known and unknown, my orishas, Yemaya, Oshun, and Shango. Buddha, Isis, Thoth, and so many other cosmic and ascended teachers, but most importantly the Divine from whom all life springs forth. Thank you for shaking me awake. Thank you for choosing me and protecting me through all of life's chaos. I am blessed beyond measure, and it is all because you all have shown me favor and love. There is never a day I am not in awe of the sun or a night where the moon isn't placed firmly outside of my window for me to gaze upon it with love. I am eternally grateful.

To the kids and bigger kids who are struggling with whom you are becoming: This Earth assignment can be rough. Please never forget that you're the coolest and smartest. Don't let anyone dim your light. I am you. Follow your heart, uncover the prayer speaking through your life, and dedicate yourself to being the best "you" possible. I'm rooting for you!

A Special Dedication to my Illustrator, Elwing Su'o'ng Gonzalez

Elwing Su'o'ng Gonzalez is a Vietnamese American teacher, artist, and author based in Los Angeles. She is most notably known on Instagram as "elwingbling" for her signature drawings of facial expressions that are usually accompanied by thoughtful and raw commentary on everything from internalized trauma to matters of race. She is also a self-published writer and illustrator of three books *It's All Within*, *A Year of Lifelong Grief*, and *Ways to Stop Killing Your Soul.*

I chose Elwing because she is the epitome of an evolving soul who isn't afraid to share her raw truths. One could even say she has cracked the code on navigating the absurd and messy the parts of life. Thank you, Elwing, for thoughtfully lending your art to help bring my feelings and human expression to life.

ABOUT ATMOSPHERE PRESS

Atmosphere Press is an independent, full-service publisher for excellent books in all genres and for all audiences. Learn more about what we do at atmospherepress.com.

We encourage you to check out some of Atmosphere's latest releases, which are available at Amazon.com and via order from your local bookstore:

The Great Unfixables, by Neil Taylor

Soused at the Manor House, by Brian Crawford

Portal or Hole: Meditations on Art, Religion, Race And The Pandemic, by Pamela M. Connell

A Walk Through the Wilderness, by Dan Conger

The House at 104: Memoir of a Childhood, by Anne Hegnauer

A Short History of Newton Hall, Chester, by Chris Fozzard

Serial Love: When Happily Ever After... Isn't, by Kathy Kay

Sit-Ins, Drive-Ins and Uncle Sam, by Bill Slawter

Black Water and Tulips, by Sara Mansfield Taber

Ghosted: Dating & Other Paramoural Experiences, by Jana Eisenstein

Walking with Fay: My Mother's Uncharted Path into Dementia, by Carolyn Testa

FLAWED HOUSES of FOUR SEASONS, by James Morris

Word for New Weddings, by David Glusker and Thom Blackstone

It's Really All about Collaboration and Creativity! A Textbook and Self-Study Guide for the Instrumental Music Ensemble Conductor, by John F. Colson

A Life of Obstructions, by Rob Penfield

Troubled Skies Over Quaker Hill: A Search for the Truth, by Lessie Auletti

ABOUT THE AUTHOR

Janine Nicole Dennis is the Owner/Chief Innovations Officer for Talent Think Innovations, LLC, a multidisciplinary management consulting firm. Her career spans over seventeen years and has taken her through the sectors of pharmaceuticals, the arts, K-12 education, technology, private equity, healthcare, staffing, and R&D just to name a few. Janine is a rare professional who isn't afraid to tackle the obstacles and issues facing us as a society and global marketplace. She has been quoted by *HBR, Thrive Global, Bustle, The Cut, Atlanta BlackStar, Newsday, SHRM, USA Today* and has been featured by *Entrepreneur, Fast Company, Black Enterprise,* and *Ebony Magazine.*

CPSIA information can be obtained
at www.ICGtesting.com
Printed in the USA
LVHW070841271122
733522LV00052B/1182/J